SPITFIRE V
VS
C.202 *FOLGORE*
Malta 1942

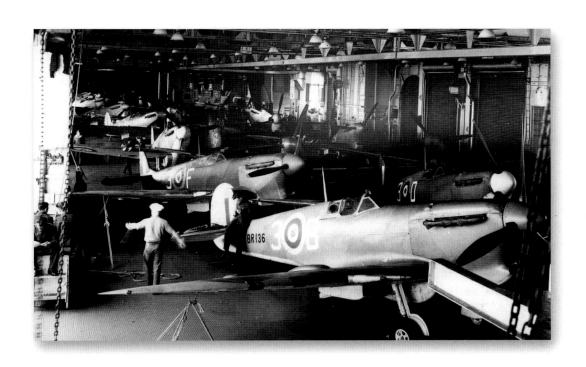

DONALD NIJBOER

First published in Great Britain in 2014 by Osprey Publishing
PO Box 883, Oxford, OX1 9PL, UK
PO Box 3985, New York, NY 10185-3985, USA
E-mail: info@ospreypublishing.com

A CIP catalogue record for this book is available from the British Library

ISBN: 978 1 78200 356 4
PDF e-book ISBN: 978 1 78200 357 1
e-Pub ISBN: 978 1 78200 358 8

Edited by Tony Holmes
Cover artworks and battlescene by Gareth Hector
Three-views, cockpits, armament scrap views and Engaging the Enemy
artwork by Jim Laurier

Index by Marie-Pierre Evans
Maps by Bounford.com
Originated by PDQ Media, Bungay, UK
Printed in China through Asia Pacific Offset Ltd.

14 15 16 17 18 10 9 8 7 6 5 4 3 2 1

Osprey Publishing is supporting the Woodland Trust, the UK's leading
woodland conservation charity, by funding the dedication of trees.

www.ospreypublishing.com

Acknowledgements

I would like to thank Dan Patterson, Giorgio Apostolo, Jacques Brunelle,
Chris Dunning, Richard J. Caruana, Wayne Ralph and Giovanni Massimello
for their assistance, along with Christopher Shores, Brian Cull and Nicola
Malizia for granting me permission to use excerpts from their book *Malta:
The Spitfire Year 1942*. Finally, thank you to my lovely partner Janet for all
of her help in the production of this volume.

Spitfire VC cover art

Future ranking Malta ace Sgt George Beurling claimed his fifth and six
victories in defence of the beleaguered island on 10 July 1942 when he
destroyed a Bf 109 and a C.202. At 1115 hrs eight Spitfires from No. 126 Sqn,
six from No. 249 Sqn and four from No. 603 Sqn were scrambled to meet a raid
comprising six Ju 88s escorted by of one *Staffel* of Bf 109s (from I./JG 77) and
a small number of C.202s from 378ª *Squadriglia*, 155° *Gruppo*. All three Spitfire
squadrons would duly make claims against the Axis aircraft, with Beurling
shooting down both a Bf 109 and a C.202. The latter aircraft was almost
certainly flown by Sergente Maggiore Francesco Visentini. Diving into a
formation of *Folgores*, Beurling (flying Spitfire VC BR323/S) singled one
out and attacked it. 'The "Eyetie" went into a steep dive, pulled out and
twisted away, rolled and pulled into a climb,' Beurling recalled. 'Finally, he
went into a loop at the end of this climb, and I nabbed him just at its top.
A two-second burst blew his cockpit apart. The pilot bailed out in a hell of a
hurry.' Visentini was subsequently rescued from the sea some three hours later
by a Cant Z.506B floatplane, having suffered wounds to his arms and legs.
His demise raised Beurling's Malta tally to six victories in just four days.
(Artwork by Gareth Hector)

C.202 *Folgore* cover art

2 July 1942 would prove to be a costly day for both sides involved in the
fighting over Malta. Axis bombing raids began at 0815hrs, and they would
continue for the next 24 hours. The combined assault involved bombers from
both the Luftwaffe and *Regia Aeronautica*, which were escorted by Bf 109Fs,
Reggiane Re.2001s and C.202s. The final daylight raid occurred between
1945hrs and 2020hrs when three Savoia-Marchetti S.84bis bombers,
with a close escort of ten C.202s led by Capitano Furio Doglio Niclot of
151ª *Squadriglia*, approached the island. Seven Spitfires of No. 249 Sqn, which
had already been scrambled, were joined by four more from No. 185 Sqn in
pursuit of the enemy formation. In the combat that followed the British pilots
claimed two C.202s shot down and three damaged. The Italians, however,
would exact a toll of their own. During a head-on attack on a C.202 that
was almost certainly flown by Capitano Niclot, the No. 249 Sqn Spitfire VC
(BR377/T-K) of Sgt C. S. G. De Nancrede was damaged to such a degree that
the pilot was forced to crash land at Takali airfield. Upon returning to his base
at Gela, on Sicily, Capitano Niclot claimed one Spitfire shot down as his first
victory over Malta. Niclot would become the leading Italian ace of the Malta
campaign, with six and three shared kills, prior to his death in combat on
27 July 1942, when he fell victim to Sgt George Beurling. (Artwork by
Gareth Hector)

CONTENTS

INTRODUCTION

Long before the Spitfire V and Macchi C.202 *Folgore* (Lightning) ever met in combat over Malta, an aerial battle for air supremacy had been fought out between Britain and Italy over the peaceful waters of the English Channel. During the celebrated Schneider Trophy races, both R. J. Mitchell and Dr Mario Castoldi would design two of the most impressive aircraft the world has ever seen. Powered by the Rolls-Royce R engine, Mitchell's Supermarine S 6B would claim the prize for Britain once and for all on

The Spitfire's ancestry can be traced directly to the Supermarine S 6B Schneider Trophy winner of 1931. Creating the seaplane, powered by a Rolls-Royce R engine, provided both Supermarine and Rolls-Royce with a sound grounding for the future development of both the Spitfire and the Merlin engine. This particular example, S1596 (the second S 6B built), broke the world air speed record on 29 September 1931 when Flt Lt George Stainforth reached 407.5mph whilst at the controls. (Crown Copyright)

13 September 1931 when the floatplane achieved a top speed of 380mph. Unfortunately for the Italians, their Macchi M.C.72 was not ready for the race and did not compete. Regarded as one of the most beautiful aircraft ever built, the sleek and graceful M.C.72 would subsequently shatter the world speed record by achieving 440mph in October 1934. No propeller-driven seaplane has ever gone any faster.

The advance in aircraft design, particularly in respect to aerodynamics and engine development, as a result of the Schneider Trophy was significant. Indeed, the creation of the Rolls-Royce R Engine (2,350hp) led directly to the famous Merlin. According to A. F. Sidgreaves, managing director of Rolls-Royce, the Schneider Trophy races compressed ten years of engine development into 24 months. Without that focus the Merlin may have never been created in time, if at all. The competition also revealed Italy's Achilles heel – engine development. The M.C.72 was in fact a twin-engined aircraft. Unable to find a single engine capable of developing the required horsepower to compete with the S 6B, Dr Castoldi coupled two Fiat AS.5 engines together to create the AS.6, which was rated at 2,300hp. It worked, but the lack of engines equal to British, German or American powerplants would limit the effectiveness of Dr Castoldi's early fighter designs.

In the end the lessons learned from the Schneider Trophy races would be seen in two of the best fighters of World War II – the Supermarine Spitfire and Macchi C.202 *Folgore*.

When Italy entered the war on 10 June 1940, the *Regia Aeronautica* was not well equipped. Its frontline fighter force consisted of just 77 operational Macchi C.200 and 88 Fiat G.50 monoplane fighters and 200 CR.42 and 177 CR.32 biplane fighters. Compared to the British Spitfire I and Hurricane I, Italy's best fighter, the C.200, was clearly no match for the frontline Royal Air Force (RAF) machines. While a well-designed fighter, the C.200 suffered from a lack of engine power – its Fiat A 74 RC38 radial engine delivered just 870hp, compared to the Rolls-Royce Merlin XII, which produced 1,140hp in the Spitfire IIA/B that was then in production.

The RAF's victory over the much-vaunted Luftwaffe during the Battle of Britain in the summer of 1940 cemented the Spitfire's place in aviation history. It was a true turning point in the war, after which Spitfires would go on to fight on every front and theatre around the world. However, the first examples of the RAF's premier fighter would not be seen in the Mediterranean until early March 1942, by which point the Spitfire V had been in service for a year.

The origins of the Mk V can be traced directly to the appearance of the Messerschmitt Bf 109F-0 over British skies in October 1940. The newly installed boss of RAF Fighter Command, Air Vice-Marshal Sholto Douglas, knew the Bf 109F was clearly superior

Although the Macchi M.C.72 was not ready to complete against the Supermarine S 6B in the Schneider Trophy in September 1931, the sleek and graceful seaplane would subsequently shatter the world speed record by achieving 440mph in October 1934. No propeller-driven seaplane has ever gone any faster. (Aermacchi)

The clean and graceful lines of the Spitfire are clearly seen here as Mk VB R6923/QJ-S of No. 92 Sqn is banked for the photographer by its pilot. Fortunately for the RAF, the Spitfire and the Rolls-Royce Merlin had considerable 'stretch' in their designs. Without that advantage the RAF would have been forced to fight on with the Hurricane II and Spitfire II while waiting for the new and 'questionable' Typhoon and Tornado fighters to enter service. Its remarkable development potential was shown by the fact that it remained in the frontline from the first day of World War II to the very last. Originally a Spitfire I, R6923 served with No. 19 Sqn and No. 7 Operational Training Unit in 1940. Converted into a Mk VB, it was shot down over the Channel by a Bf 109 on 22 June 1941. (Author)

to the Spitfire I and demanded a quick fix. A stopgap Spitfire was urgently needed, and Rolls-Royce and Supermarine came up with the answer in the form of the Mk V. By taking the existing Mk I airframe and simply adding the new Merlin 45/46 engine (rated at 1,470hp), the Spitfire V was born and the balance redressed.

For the Italians the problem was similar. Roughly equal to the Hurricane I in terms of its performance (although considerably less well armed), the C.200 was nevertheless clearly obsolete by 1940. In the spring of 1940 Dr Mario Castoldi, well aware of the C.200's radial engine limitations, arranged for the importation of the German liquid-cooled Daimler-Benz DB 601A-1 engine rated at 1,175hp. The prototype Macchi fighter combined the wings, undercarriage and vertical and horizontal tail units of the C.200 with a new fuselage, to which was fitted the imported DB 601A-1 engine.

Designated the C.202, the new machine was a thoroughbred. Its speed, finger-light handling qualities and superb agility would make it the *Regia Aeronautica's* most outstanding fighter of the war. Introduced in the summer of 1941, the C.202 was clearly superior to the Hurricane and Curtiss Tomahawk and Kittyhawk – the fighter types then in service with the RAF in North Africa and the Mediterranean. The Macchi could out-turn any of its opponents, and it was equal to, and in some respects better than, the Spitfire V.

The history of these two fighters will forever be linked with the savage air battles that took place over the skies of Malta in 1942. By the spring of that year Malta had been under siege for almost two years. The *Regia Aeronautica*, unable to subdue the island's defences since June 1940, was joined by the Luftwaffe for a second time in January 1942. This time, German and Italian units were equipped with two of their best fighters, the Bf 109F and the new C.202. The RAF could muster just three squadrons of Hurricane IIs, which were completely outclassed. Incredibly, there were 80 squadrons of Spitfires based in England at this time, but not one in the Mediterranean or North Africa. Malta was considered a backwater by the RAF, but it soon became apparent that without Spitfires it would surely fall.

The situation facing the embattled defenders was grimly summarized by the new CO of No. 249 Sqn, 10.5-victory ace Sqn Ldr Stan Turner, in a note to Air Vice-Marshal Sir Hugh Lloyd, Air Officer Commanding Malta, in February 1942:

Either, sir, we get the Spitfires here within days, not weeks, or we're done. That's it.

Finally, on 7 March 1942, the first 15 of many Spitfire Vs were flown off the carrier HMS *Eagle* bound for Malta. More would follow, and by 20 April 91 Mk Vs had been delivered. Their arrival coincided with the appearance of Italian fighters over Malta for the first time in nearly three months. Prior to this, the RAF had been almost exclusively duelling with aircraft of the Luftwaffe. On 2 April 4° *Stormo* C.T. (a *Stormo* comprised 72 aircraft in three *gruppi*, with each *gruppo* being made up of two *squadriglie* equipped with 12 aircraft each) flew to Sicily equipped with 26 new C.202s. Its first mission was flown on 20 April when 19 C.202s of 10° *Gruppo* flew a fighter sweep over Malta. No Spitfires were encountered, but two C.202s were lost when they collided in flight and crashed.

For the next six months pilots flying Spitfire Vs and C.202s would battle it out over the skies of Malta. It was a struggle between two of the most evenly matched fighters to see combat during World War II.

Seeing how World War II-era fighters compared is not a simple numbers game. While speed, rate-of-climb, diving speed, armament and manoeuvrability were vital factors, they do not tell the whole story. In the end what made a fighter victorious was a combination of technology, tactics, leadership, pilot training, industrial prowess, serviceability and sound doctrine. It was these factors that would determine the fate of the Spitfire V and C.202.

Fresh from the factory floor, this C.202 (Serie III MM7806) is painted in the regulation scheme specified for operations in the 'colonies'. The overall base colour was Giallo Mimetico (yellow), with Verde Mimetico (green) mottling, and Nocciola Chiaro (light chestnut) undersides. Macchi built 140 Serie III *Folgores* from May 1941 through to April 1942. This is a late-build aircraft, identified by the ribbed tropical dust filter on the supercharger intake. The 'AS' designation stencilled on the rear fuselage beneath the military serial identifies this particular machine as being a C.202AS (*Africa Settentrionale*), as per the tropical modifications. (Author)

CHRONOLOGY

1931
13 September   Supermarine S 6B takes the Schneider Trophy prize with a top speed of 380mph.

1934
October   The M.C.72 floatplane claims the world speed record with a top speed of 440mph.

1 December   The British Air Ministry issues a contract for the new Mitchell-designed Rolls-Royce Merlin-powered monoplane fighter that would evolve into the Spitfire.

1936
5 March   Spitfire prototype K5054, powered by a Rolls-Royce Merlin C engine, flies for the first time, taking off from Eastleigh airfield.

June   The first contract for 310 Spitfire Is is signed by Vickers-Supermarine and the Air Ministry.

1937
24 December   The Macchi C.200 prototype, flown by Gisueppe Burei, takes to the air for the first time.

1938
14 May   Spitfire I makes its maiden flight.

August   No. 19 Sqn is the first RAF unit to be equipped with the new Spitfire I.

1939
June   C.200 series production gets underway.

1940
Spring   Dr Mario Castoldi privately approaches Daimler-Benz to arrange for the importation of the 12-cylinder liquid-cooled DB 601A-1. Simultaneously, he begins work on adapting the basic C.200 airframe to accept the German powerplant.

10 June   Italy declares war on Great Britain. Twenty-four hours later 33 bombers from the *Regia Aeronautica* launch the first raids on Malta.

August   Official negotiations begin for the purchase of Daimler-Benz engines for installation in the first batch of C.202s. Alfa Romeo receives approval to licence build the DB 601A-1 as the RA 1000 RC41-I *Monsone* (Monsoon).

10 August   Prototype C.202 (MM445) powered by a DB 601A-1 engine takes to the air.

December   Spitfire V prototype (K9788), powered by a Merlin 45 engine developing 1,470hp, makes its maiden flight.

9 December   Gen Archibald Wavell launches the first British ground offensive against Italian forces in Egypt.

1941
February   First units of the *Africa Korps* under Generalleutnant Erwin Rommel start to arrive in Libya during Operation *Sonnenblume*.

June   Six RAF fighter squadrons are fully equipped or in the process of converting to the Spitfire V.

July   First production C.202s, from the Macchi-built Serie II and III, are delivered.

| **October** | Force K is formed on Malta. Made up of ships, submarines and aircraft, this Strike Force begins offensive operations against Axis shipping bound for North Africa. |
| **December** | *Luflotte* 2, under the command of General Feldmarshall Albert Kesselring, is transferred from the Russian Front to Sicily in preparation for a new offensive against Malta. |

1942

13 February	Adolf Hitler approves Operation *Hercules*, the proposed invasion of Malta.
7 March	Fifteen Spitfire Vs fly to Malta from the aircraft carrier HMS *Eagle*.
2 April	4° *Stormo* C.T., 10° *Gruppo* arrives in Sicily with 26 C.202s, followed shortly thereafter by the similarly equipped 9° *Gruppo*.
20 April	Operation *Calendar* begins, which sees 47 Spitfire VCs take off from the carrier USS *Wasp* – 46 are safely delivered. The first fighter sweep by 19 C.202s of 10° *Gruppo* takes place over Malta.
21 April	The first C.202 victory over a Spitfire is claimed by Sottotenente Luigi Giannella from 10° *Gruppo*.
May	Malta now has five squadrons fully equipped with Spitfire Vs (Nos. 126, 185, 249, 601 and 603 Sqns).
8 May	Sgt Wilbert Dodd of No. 185 Sqn claims the first C.202 'probably destroyed'.
9 May	Operation *Bowery* begins. The carriers USS *Wasp* and HMS *Eagle* launch 64 Spitfires bound for Malta – 61 arrive safely.
10 May	Axis units suffer heavy losses over Malta. With 50 Spitfires now available, the RAF shoots down five Ju 88s, four Ju 87s, three Bf 109s, one Cant Z.1007bis and one C.202 for the loss of three Spitfires.
18 May	Axis air strength on Sicily is significantly reduced in preparation for Rommel's new desert offensive. 4° *Stormo* C.T. is ordered to Libya, its place being taken by 51° *Stormo* with 33 new C.202s.
1–14 August	Operation *Pedestal* sees the largest ever convoy despatched from Gibraltar to Malta. Only five out of fourteen transport vessels get through to the besieged island.
11 October	The final aerial blitz of Malta begins. 53° and 4° *Stormi* muster a total of 74 C.202s for the assault. By 18 October the Axis concede defeat, however.
8 November	Operation *Torch* begins, with US and British troops invading Vichy French North Africa. The siege of Malta ends. Between March and October 1942, 367 Spitfires have been successfully delivered to Malta.

The C.202 would be the most widely produced Italian single-seat fighter of the war. The first unit to be equipped with the aircraft was 17° *Gruppo* of 1° *Stormo* in May 1941. Combat capability was not achieved by the unit, however, until the autumn. By that time the *Folgore* had already seen action over Malta. This C.202 belongs to 90ª *Squadriglia*, 10° *Gruppo*, 4° *Stormo* based at Gela, on Sicily, in May 1942. (Author)

DESIGN AND DEVELOPMENT

SPITFIRE

The Supermarine Spitfire was one of the greatest fighters of World War II. Famous for its speed and manoeuvrability, its greatest attribute, however, had nothing to do with its exceptional performance. Reflected in R. J. Mitchell's brilliant design was the capacity for continued development. Long before the Battle of Britain, Supermarine was hard at work looking to improve the Spitfire through increased engine power and a strengthened airframe. Incredibly, the British Air Staff, under Air Chief Marshal Sir Cyril Newall, had initially been reluctant when it came to instigating an improved Spitfire programme. Believing the RAF's future lay with the twin-engined Westland Whirlwind and the new Hawker Tornado and Typhoon, the Air Ministry shied away from further Spitfire development.

Fortunately for the RAF the Spitfire was a proven commodity. By the spring of 1940 the Whirlwind, Tornado and Typhoon prototypes were plagued with technical problems. The Tornado's performance was disappointing and the type never went into production. The Peregrine-powered Whirlwind was underpowered and less manoeuvrable than the Spitfire, resulting in only 112 examples being built, and the Typhoon's performance as an interceptor at medium to high altitudes was also disappointing in comparison with that of the Spitfire – the fighter it was supposed to replace.

The combined lack of success with the Whirlwind, Tornado and Typhoon gave the Spitfire a new lease of life. Joe Smith, Supermarine's chief designer, had never doubted the Spitfire's ability to 'see us through the war'. Ernest Hives, head of Rolls-Royce's Aero Engine Division, was also equally dismissive of the new fighters as he knew that the Merlin had yet to reach its full potential. Near the end of 1939 Hives began work on upgrading the Merlin II into the Merlin XX. Run on 100-octane fuel, as opposed to the 85-octane in operational use at that time, and fitted with a two-speed supercharger, the new engine produced 1,390hp – the Merlin II was rate at 1,030hp.

Supermarine was also refining the Spitfire airframe, cleaning up its lines and making it ready to accommodate the heavier engine. The fuselage was slightly lengthened, the undercarriage strengthened and the tail wheel was made retractable. Impressed by the new variant, the Air Ministry ordered a prototype and designated it the Mk III (Serial N3297). Flown by Jeffrey Quill on 16 March 1940, the Spitfire III was judged 'satisfactory' in trials.

Incredibly, the Air Ministry was still unsure about the Spitfire's future. During a conference in early 1940 the subject of Fighter Command's future equipment with either the Spitfire III or Typhoon I was discussed, and the Air Ministry voiced a preference for the latter. The Battle of Britain, however, would solidify the Spitfire's reputation and future development. A strong advocate of the aeroplane was Lord Beaverbrook, Minister of Aircraft Production. With his advocacy, attitudes towards the Spitfire quickly changed, and in October 1940 1,000 Mk IIIs were ordered.

Parallel to this development was the creation of a new type of Rolls-Royce engine that was considerably more powerful than the Merlin. Known as the Griffon, it incorporated technology that was used in the famous 'R' powerplant fitted in Mitchell's famous Schneider Trophy floatplane racers. The Griffon was a big leap forward. Although slightly larger than the Merlin, it could still be mounted to the Spitfire airframe without the latter having to be significantly redesigned. Supermarine estimated that the new fighter would boast a top speed of 420mph. In May 1940 a formal contract was issued for the production of two prototypes, known as Mk IVs. In November 1941 the first prototype (DP845) took to the air, with impressive results.

More than a year earlier, the Battle of Britain had proven the Spitfire I and II to be the right fighters at the right time. Designed as a pure interceptor, the Spitfire, when married with Britain's integrated radar air defence system, performed brilliantly. Indeed, without it the battle may have been lost. A veteran of the fighting in 1940, New Zealand Spitfire ace Al Deere wrote:

> There can be no doubt that victory in the Battle of Britain was made possible by the Spitfire. Although there were more Hurricanes than Spitfires in the Battle, the Spitfire was the RAF's primary weapon because of its better all-round capability. The Hurricane alone could not have won this great air battle, but the Spitfire could have done so.

The numbers speak for themselves. Recent research and in-depth analysis by authors John Alcon and Dilip Sarkar reveal the Spitfire's true effectiveness during the Battle of Britain. The 30 squadrons of Hurricanes claimed 656 aircraft shot down, of which 222 were Bf 109s. The 19 squadrons of Spitfires, however, were credited with 529 Luftwaffe aircraft, of which no fewer than 282 were Bf 109s. As these figures

SPITFIRE VC

29ft 11in

BRI30 T⊙D

12ft 7.75in

36ft 10in

show, the Spitfire was more than a match for the Luftwaffe's principal fighter type, hence the fact Fighter Command tasked units equipped with the Supermarine aircraft to engage Bf 109s escorting German bombers, leaving the latter for the more numerous Hurricanes whenever possible.

At the beginning of the Battle of Britain the RAF was equipped with 19 squadrons of Spitfire Is. Production of the Mk I had commenced in April 1938 and it continued until March 1941, by which time 1,567 examples had been built. By June 1940 the Spitfire II had begun to appear. The new Mk II was powered by the Merlin XII, which produced 1,175hp. Top speed for the Mk II increased to 370mph, making the aircraft 15mph faster than the Spitfire I. Rate-of-climb was also improved to the tune of 473ft a minute more than the Mk I. Furthermore, the new engine was fitted with a Coffman automatic starter, thus reducing the amount of time it took to get the aircraft up and running and off the ground. Deliveries of the first Spitfire IIAs began in late August 1940, and by October 195 had been delivered.

Progress on the new Mks III and IV was slow, however. In the autumn of 1940 the Merlin XX engine was in short supply, its two-speed supercharger making the powerplant more complex to manufacture. And in an effort to keep the Hurricane competitive on the Channel front, the Air Ministry decided that the revised Mk II should receive the Merlin XX ahead of the Spitfire III. At the same time developments in Germany would force the RAF's hand when it came to acquiring a new Spitfire variant.

At the beginning of October 1940 three new Bf 109F-0 pre-production machines were delivered for service evaluation by the Luftwaffe on the Channel front. Compared to the Bf 109E, the new *'Friedrich'* featured a cleaner aerodynamic shape and a more powerful engine. It had a top speed of 373mph at 19,700ft and a service ceiling of 36,100ft, making it clearly superior to the Spitfire II. Fighter Command reacted quickly. Air Vice-Marshal Sholto Douglas, head of Fighter Command, wrote an urgent letter to Lord Beaverbrook, stating:

> I am concerned about the inferiority in the performance of our fighter aircraft compared with newer types of enemy fighters. The improved '109 not only out-climbs our fighters from about 25,000ft but it is faster at altitude and has a better ceiling. This confers the tactical initiative on the enemy.

Critically, the Spitfire III (the variant originally intended to replace the Mks I and II) was not ready. Getting it into full production was also proving difficult, as converting existing productions lines would involve considerable retooling and a great deal of time – something the RAF did not have. The Merlin XX, which featured a redesigned supercharger with separate blowers for high altitude and low altitude flying, was a complicated engine, and one Rolls-Royce could not build in sufficient numbers. Something had to be done, and quickly.

In October 1940 Rolls-Royce and Supermarine turned to the Merlin 45 (and later 46) engine. Developed in parallel with the Merlin XX by Rolls-Royce, it was effectively a simplified version of the new engine with the low altitude blower deleted. Developing 1,515hp with +16lb boost at 11,000ft, the new Merlin 45 was no larger than earlier variants of the engine, which meant that it could be easily fitted into existing Spitfire I/II airframes. The Merlin 45 was also easier to mass-produce than the Merlin XX.

A great deal of the Rolls-Royce Merlin's success during World War II came from the exceptional design of its supercharger, seen at the left end of the engine in this photograph. While the German DB 601 engine had a capacity of 33.93 litres, the Merlin's was a mere 26 litres, and it would remain this size for the entire war. The ability of Rolls-Royce to progressively improve the power of the Merlin through supercharger design and higher-octane fuel took the engine's rating from 1,000hp at the start of the war to 2,300hp in 1945. The Merlin 45, seen here, is equipped with a single-stage, single-speed supercharger. The Spitfire V and Seafire IB, IIC and III would be powered by the Merlin 45, 45M, 46, 50, 50A, 50M, 55 and 55M series of engines. (Author)

Rolls-Royce soon received instructions to re-engine 23 Spitfire Is, thus creating the first Mk Vs.

In January 1941 flight trials of the new fighter commenced, and these went so well that the more complex Mks III and IV were ultimately dropped and the Spitfire V was rushed into production. Early build Mk Vs were effectively Spitfire I and IIA/B (the A was armed with eight 0.303-in. Browning machine guns, while the B boasted a pair of 20mm Hispano cannon and four 0.303-in. Brownings) airframes fitted with Merlin 45 engines. The heavier weight of the new engine and additional equipment added extra stress to the original Spitfire I airframes, which in turn limited their operational capabilities. Production of the Spitfire VC from early October 1941 rectified these problems, however, through the introduction of a significant number of improvements to the fighter.

During the Battle of Britain Spitfire pilots had found that high-speed combat above 400mph caused the fighter's ailerons to lock up. A great deal of strength needed to be exerted in order to get any kind of movement out of the machine in the rolling plane. The problem was soon isolated – high-speed airflow over the fabric-covered ailerons caused them to balloon out, leaving them ineffective. The solution was a simple one – replace the fabric with a light alloy. Another problem that frustrated the young Spitfire pilots was the enemy's ability to simply dive out of trouble. The Bf 109E's fuel injection system was superior to the Spitfire's float-type carburettor, which caused the engine to cut out during any negative G manoeuvre. Anti-G modifications to the SU carburettor soon rectified the problem, and this 'fix' was subsequently fitted to the new Merlin 45/46 engine.

When the time came to send notoriously short-ranged Spitfires to Malta, a two-part solution had to be found to the problem of getting the aircraft to the island. Early in 1940 Hurricanes had been successfully launched off an aircraft carrier and flown

to Malta. Replicating this feat with a Spitfire V meant a 660-mile one-way flight, which was far in excess of the fighter's range. To address the problem, Supermarine developed the 90-gallon jettisonable slipper tank. The drop tank proved successful, and subsequent Spitfire VBs and VCs were equipped with the necessary plumbing to accept the store.

The new Spitfire V would also have to be tropicalized for the conditions on Malta. The fine dust it would encounter was an engine killer, for sand entering the Merlin caused excess wear, lower power output and a shortened lifespan. To battle the dust, the Vokes filter was added. Housed in a beard-like faring under the fighter's nose, it was not popular with pilots. While the filter reduced the Mk V's top speed, its benefits far outweighed any reduction in performance caused by excessive wear. Other tropical items were also added. Fitted in the rear fuselage behind the cockpit was a tank for 1.5 gallons of drinking water, along with a container of flying rations, an emergency tool roll, emergency equipment and a signal pistol with cartridges.

The Spitfire V also introduced the new C-Type or 'Universal' wing. The original A-type wing design carried eight 0.303-in. Browning machine guns with 300 rounds per gun. The B-type was modified to carry two 20mm drum-fed Hispano Mk II cannons with 60 rounds per gun, plus four 0.303-in. Brownings. The C-wing was structurally modified to reduce the amount of effort required to rearm the weapons and to allow for the fitment of a combination of mixed armament – A-type, B-type or four 20mm cannon. The ammunition supply for the latter was doubled to 120 rounds per gun. The first Spitfire Vs were A-models armed with eight 0.303-in. Browning machine guns. They were followed by cannon-armed Mk VBs and VCs.

The rush to get the Spitfire V into service meant that early machines suffered a number of faults. Normally considered a reliable aircraft, the Mk V soon began to show its vicious side. According to Jeffrey Quill more than 20 Spitfires (mostly

Well-weathered Spitfire VB BM635/WZ-Y, seen here with a Piper L-4 Grasshopper, was assigned to the USAAF's 309th Fighter Sqadron/31st Fighter Group. Part of a 1,000-strong Mk VB order placed by the Air Ministry with Vickers-Armstrongs and constructed in the company's Castle Bromwich plant between November 1941 and November 1942, this aircraft was issued new to the USAAF fighter unit at High Ercall, in Shropshire, in June 1942. The most noticeable features of the Spitfire VB can be seen here. The first is the B-type wing, fitted with two 20mm Hispano cannons and four 0.303-in. Browning machine guns. The fishtail exhausts stubs replaced the early ejector type and a new wide-blade Rotol constant speed propeller was fitted instead of the de Havilland unit. The blades were made of compressed wood and the spinner was longer and more pointed. BM635 would subsequently serve with Nos. 65 and 345 Sqns and No. 61 OTU before being struck off charge on 13 February 1945. (Author)

Spitfire VC Trop BR226 was photographed just after being loaded onto the aircraft carrier USS *Wasp* (CV-7), moored in Glasgow Harbour's King George V docks, as part of Operation *Calendar* in early April 1942. Painted in the factory-applied desert colours of Middle Stone/Dark Earth, with Sky Blue undersides, the fighter is equipped with a full armament of four 20mm cannon and eight 0.303-in. machine guns. Note the 'missing' wingtips crammed into the Spitfire's open cockpit. BR226 would be lost in combat with Bf 109Fs over Malta on 4 May 1942, resulting in the death of its pilot, eight-victory ace Flt Lt Norman MacQueen of No. 249 Sqn. (Author)

Mk VBs) broke apart in the air due to mainframe or engine failure. The airframe failures were traced to longitudinal instability. This was due largely to the shift in the centre of gravity towards the rear of the aeroplane. New equipment, of course, meant more weight, and by 1943 a study carried out by the Royal Aircraft Establishment at Farnborough showed that the average speed of a late production Mk V was slower than the original Mk I!

While RAF Fighter Command redressed the balance with the 'stop gap' Spitfire V in early 1941, the Fleet Air Arm would also benefit from the development of this variant. Desperate for a single-engined carrier fighter with the performance to match the fabled Spitfire, the British Admiralty demanded the creation of a navalised version of the aeroplane. The first Spitfire to be 'hooked' was Mk VB BL676 in late 1941, and after encouraging carrier trials 250 Mk VBs and VCs were earmarked for conversion.

The Mk V would have the longest combat career of all the Spitfire variants to see action during World War II. Even after the Mk V had been superseded by the Mk IX as a high-altitude fighter, the variant found a new role as a low-altitude fighter. Fitted with a Merlin optimized for low-level work, the LF V would equip 11 squadrons assigned to the Air Defence of Great Britain (ADGB) as late as June 1944. And the Mk V (in Seafire form) would also be involved in one of the last dogfights of World War II. On 15 August 1945 a mixed formation of eight Seafire L IIIs and F IIIs encountered four Imperial Japanese Navy Mitsubishi J2M3 Raidens and eight Mitsubishi A6M5c and A6M7 Zero-sens over Tokyo Bay. The result was seven Zero-sens shot down for the loss of one Seafire.

Even with its faults, the Spitfire V would prove to be the right fighter at the right time. Its speed, armament and ceiling gave the aeroplane the edge it would need in the skies over Malta. In total 6,472 Mk Vs were built – 94 Mk VAs by Supermarine, 3,911 Mk VBs (776 by Supermarine, 2,995 at Castle Bromwich and 140 by Westland) and 2,467 Mk VCs (478 by Supermarine, 1,494 by Castle Bromwich and 495 by Westland).

C.202 *FOLGORE*

The Macchi C.202 has to be regarded as one of the finest fighters of World War II. Often forgotten and mentioned in only passing, Dr Mario Castoldi's aircraft garnered the highest respect from Allied pilots – something wartime propaganda tried to play down. Initially viewed as a forced marriage between a German engine and existing Italian airframe, the C.202 was not taken seriously. This sentiment quickly vanished when Hurricane and Kittyhawk pilots found themselves fighting for their lives against the fast and nimble C.202.

Long before Italy entered the war, the *Regia Aeronautica* was beset by a number of serious problems. Having established numerous world records during the 1920s and 1930s, Italian aviation was held in high regard across the globe. From 1936 to 1939 Italian fighters and bombers fought with great success against the Republican forces during the Spanish Civil War. European countries like Sweden, Hungary, Belgium and Finland considered the Italians to be leaders in military aviation, and were eager to buy their fighter designs (Fiat CR.42s and G.50s and Reggiane Re.2000s). Unfortunately for the Italians, such success bred self-satisfaction within its aviation industry, which effectively ignored what was happening in the rest of Europe, Japan and the United States.

Not all Italians were completely unaware of the situation abroad, however. In 1939 a series of more modern fighters began to enter service with the *Regia Aeronautica*, but their performance, while a step up from the previous generation of biplane fighters (CR.32 and CR.42), did not live up to world standards. This meant that both the Fiat G.50 and Macchi C.200 monoplane fighters were virtually obsolete by the time they entered service in 1938 and 1939, respectively. The culprit was engine power. Both were powered by the 870hp Fiat A 74 RC38 air-cooled radial engine that had

The Macchi C.200 *Saetta* would provide the foundation for Dr Mario Castoldi's next fighter, the C.202. Although a joy for its pilots to fly (like the majority of Italian fighters in World War II) thanks to it being highly manoeuvrable and light on the controls, the C.200 was both underpowered and under-armed. (Author)

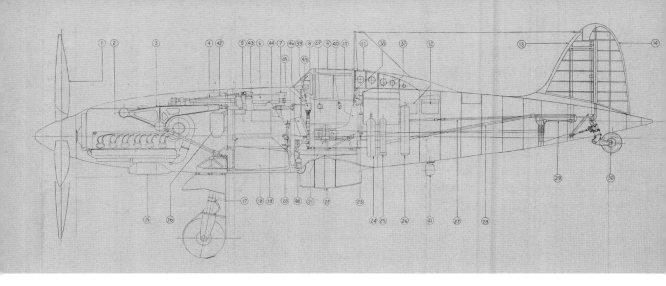

The graceful and well-proportioned lines of the C.202 can be clearly seen in this factory-produced side-view cutaway drawing. The *Folgore's* internal components reveal a well-balanced and compact design. While it lacked a heavy-hitting armament, the C.202 was well armoured, with good protection for the pilot in the form of a moulded, handmade armour-plated seat (which was somewhat lighter than comparable Allied seats) and self-sealing fuel tanks. The aircraft lacked laminated, bulletproof, glass in the windscreen, however. (Author)

previously been fitted to the CR.42. The only Italian fighter with respectable performance was the Reggiane Re.2000. First flown in 1938, the Re.2000, powered by a Piaggo P XI RC40 radial engine rated at 870hp, attained a maximum speed of 320mph. Just 17 examples were ordered by the *Regia Aeronautica*, although the Re.2000 enjoyed greater export success.

All three fighters were considerably underpowered when compared to their liquid-cooled inline-engined contemporaries such as the Hurricane I, Spitfire I and Bf 109E. In an effort to address this problem *Il Duce*, Benito Mussolini, forced the resignation of the Chief of the Air Staff in late 1939 and installed Francesco Pricolo in his place. By then a homegrown liquid-cooled engine known as the Fiat A38 was two years into development, but it was struggling to match the performance of rival powerplants from Britain and Germany. Frustrated by this, Dr Mario Castoldi privately approached Daimler-Benz AG and arranged for the importation of the highly successful DB 601A-1 engine in the spring of 1940. His plan was to marry the 1,175hp motor with a modified C.200 airframe.

Castoldi's C.200 *Saetta* (Thunderbolt) was Italy's first truly modern fighter. An all-metal machine, the C.200 was a cantilever low-wing monoplane with hydraulically retractable landing gear and a partially enclosed all-round cockpit canopy. Compared to the Spitfire and Bf 109, the C.200 did not share their clean, elegant, lines, but it did have exceptional manoeuvrability. It was also a stable gun platform and its handling was finger-light under all conditions. The Macchi was powered by the ubiquitous Fiat A 74 RC38 14-cylinder two-row geared and supercharged air-cooled radial engine, which produced 870hp at 2,520rpm for take off and 840hp at 12,500ft. Top speed was 312mph at 14,750ft. Armed with just two Breda-SAFAT 12.7mm machine guns firing through the propeller arc, the C.200 was at an extreme disadvantage when up against Allied fighters that boasted at least six (and often eight) 0.303-in. machine guns.

The first Daimler-Benz engine reached Macchi's Varese factory in the spring of 1940. The marriage of the DB 601 engine to the modified C.200 airframe (the C.202 had a redesigned forward fuselage section, but retained the C.200's wings, landing gear and vertical tail and tailplanes) radically changed the appearance of the fighter. The once-graceful symmetry that had characterized Castoldi's high-speed floatplanes reappeared. Featuring with the C.200's outstanding flying characteristics and powered by the DB 601 engine, the prototype (MM445) took to the air on 10 August 1940. Macchi test pilot Comandante Guido Carestiato declared it an unqualified success, and following initial approval the *Ministero dell'Aeronautica* issued an immediate instruction for series production. The Daimler-Benz engine was also put into production under licence by Alfa Romeo as the RA 1000 RC41-I *Monsone* (Monsoon) rated at 1,075hp at 2,500rpm for take off.

Production of the C.202 *Folgore* was shared between the Macchi plant at Varese, Breda's facility at Sesto San Giovanni and SAI-Ambrosini at Passignano. Just eight months after signing the first production contract, C.202s began rolling off the assembly lines. It was at this point that the weakness of the Italian aircraft industry began to be revealed once again. Production rates for the C.202 were extremely low, resulting in between 1,150 and 1,200 examples being built in two years. By comparison, the British produced 6,487 Spitfire Vs alone during the same period.

The reasons behind Italy's anaemic production rates were many and varied. Despite every effort being made by the Italian aircraft industry to boost productivity, the number of new C.202s available to the *Regia Aeronautica* was continually restricted by a shortage of powerplants. Supplies of raw materials, for which Italy was dependant on Germany, were not always available either. These shortages, combined with the enforced emigration of skilled workers to German factories, kept *Folgore* production well below the essential minimum for sustained combat operations. The C.202 also required 20,000 man-hours to produce compared to just 4,500 for the Bf 109.

As the first C.202s began to leave the production lines in mid-1941, these aircraft differed little from the original prototype. Indeed, the only modifications made were extending the supercharger air intake, deletion of the glazed panelling aft of the pilot's seat and the replacement of the retractable tailwheel with a fixed unit. The RA 1000 RC41-I engine drove a 9ft 10.333in three-bladed Piaggio P.1001 metal airscrew.

Like its European counterparts, the C.202 had cockpit armour plating for the pilot and self-sealing fuel tanks. Armament, however, was meagre at best. The two

Factory-fresh Serie III C.202 MM7762, which was one of 140 *Folgores* constructed by Macchi between May 1941 and April 1942. Production examples differed from the prototype by having indentations in the headrest fairing for improved rear vision, a fixed tailwheel and a long supercharger intake, which replaced the original square version. The first production C.202s were powered by 400+ DB 601A-1 engines, which were supplied used from Luftwaffe stocks. The first licence-built *Monsone* versions did not come off the Alfa Romeo production line until the summer of 1941. [Author]

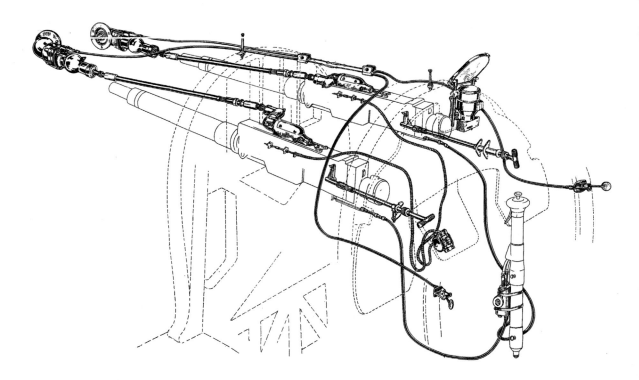

Armed with just two Breda-SAFAT 12.7mm machine guns, the C.202 was one of the mostly lightly armed fighters of World War II. To make matters even worse, both guns were synchronized to fire through the propeller arc, reducing the weapons' rate-of-fire. The latter would vary from 380 up to 750 rounds per minute, depending on the speed at which the propeller was rotating. (Author)

Breda-SAFAT 12.7mm machine guns with 370 to 400 rounds per weapon were mounted on top of the engine and synchronized to fire through the propeller. This limited their rate-of-fire to just 575 rounds per minute, and it could be lower depending on the engine's rpm. To makes matters worse, the Breda-SAFAT machine gun was not one of the best aerial weapons of World War II. While the Breda-SAFATs were reliable and accurate, they had the worst power-to-weight ratio in terms of shell destructiveness of all aircraft machine guns. The two-gun armament of the C.202 was clearly inadequate.

Surprisingly, after 400 fighters had been built the armament issue was finally addressed, but with only modest results. A single Breda-SAFAT 7.7mm machine gun, with 500 rounds per weapon, was installed in each wing. These guns were too small to be effective, and instead of adding more firepower the modification simply increased the all-up weight of the fighter. Compared to the Spitfire VB's two Hispano 20mm cannon and four Browning 0.303-in. machine guns, the C.202 was at a distinct disadvantage.

A San Giorgio Type B reflector gunsight and Allocchio Bacchini B.30 R/T were standard equipment. A moulded armour-plate seat was also fitted (it was somewhat lighter than comparable Allied seats), but no armoured windscreen was included.

As production began to ramp up, the original prototype was tested extensively at the Guidonia Experimental Centre. It had a take-off weight of 6,206lb and achieved speeds of 304mph at sea level, 319mph at 3,280ft, 334mph at 6,560ft, 349mph at 9,840ft, 362mph at 13,120ft and 372mph at 16,405ft. Climbing trials also revealed some very impressive numbers – 3,280ft in 34 seconds, 6,560ft in 1 min 19 sec, 9,840ft in 2 min 26 sec, 13,200ft in 3 min 27 sec and 16,405ft in 4 min 40 sec. All this was accomplished with an engine that had 340 less horsepower than the Merlin 45/46. The production model, with a take-off weight of 6,415lb (just 209lb more), was only fractionally slower than the prototype.

C.202 *FOLGORE*

29ft 0.5in

9ft 11.5in

34ft 8in

C.202 Serie VII MM9042 was the personal aircraft of Capt Furio Doglio Niclot, CO of 151ª *Squadrigilia*, 20° *Gruppo*, 51° *Stormo* based at Gela during June 1942. MM9042 had been ferried from Macchi to Ciampino on 16 June 1942, and then on to Gela eight days later. Incredibly, in just 12 days, Capitano Niclot achieved six victories over Malta while flying this aircraft before being shot down in it by Malta ace George Beurling on 27 July 1942. The fighter boasted a rare white command pennant forward of 51° *Stormo's* famous 'black cat and green mice' emblem.

The addition of the DB 601 engine transformed Mario Castoldi's original C.200 fighter into a true thoroughbred. It would also benefit another fighter – the Reggiane Re.2001 *Ariete I* (Ram). Like the C.200, the original Re.2000 was powered by an air-cooled radial engine that gave it a top speed of 329mph at 16,400ft. When married to the DB 601A-1, the new Re.2001 had a top speed of 339mph at 17,954ft. Experiencing the same problems as Macchi when it came to acquiring RA 1000 RC41 engines, Reggiane only succeeded in building 237 Re.2001s. During the deadly dogfights over Malta in 1942 Spitfire V pilots often mistook the Re.2001 for the C.202.

The C.202's production run was short – from mid-1941 through to August 1943. Further production was stopped when a new Italian government signed an armistice agreement with the Allies the following month. The fighters were built in 13 production series, but this did not necessarily mean there was a modification or equipment change in each series. In fact relatively few modifications were made to the C.202 during its production.

The first unit of the *Regia Aeronautica* to convert to the C.202 was 17° *Gruppo*, 1° *Stormo Caccia Terrestre* (C.T.), based at Campoformido near Udine. Aircraft were delivered from May 1941, but the unit did not reach operational combat status until the autumn. By that time the *Folgore* had already seen action with 9° *Gruppo* over Malta, this unit having received its first C.202s in July 1941. After a two-month work-up period as part of 4° *Stormo* C.T., 9° *Gruppo* was transferred to Sicily in September. On the last day of that same month Tenente Jacopo Frigerio of 97ª *Squadriglia* claimed the C.202's first aerial victory when he shot down a Hurricane IIB fighter-bomber of No. 185 Sqn that had attacked the unit's base at Comiso.

For the first time in the war the *Regia Aeronautica* had a fighter that was better than the RAF's Hurricane II and Kittyhawk (although not in respect to their armament). However, although it was equal to the Spitfire V in terms of performance, it lacked the heavier firepower of the Supermarine fighter. As with the Spitfire, the *Folgore* had room for improvement.

Not content with resting on his laurels, Dr Mario Castoldi produced the C.205V *Veltro* (Greyhound), which flew for the first time on 19 April 1942. Using the same

When paired with the German DB 601A-1 liquid-cooled engine, the C.200 was transformed into the superlative C.202. The Daimler-Benz motor was a remarkably clean, uncluttered powerplant, being an excellent example of German engineering at its most efficient. As previously noted, early production C.202s were powered by used German engines. This directly affected serviceability rates, greatly reducing the combat effectiveness of the *Folgore*. (Author)

C.202 airframe, the aircraft was powered by a Fiat-built version of the Daimler-Benz DB 605A-1 engine known as the RA 1050 RC58 *Tifone* (Typhoon) rated at 1,475hp. The prototype attained a maximum speed of 399mph at 26,620ft. Again, its armament initially consisted of just two 12.7mm and two 7.7mm Breda-SAFAT machine guns, but with development of the Serie III variant came the fitment of more powerful Mauser MG 151 20mm cannon, with 250 rounds per gun, in place of the wing-mounted 7.7mm weapons. Underwing racks could also be fitted for the carriage of two 110lb, 220lb or 353lb bombs.

Dr Castoldi considered the C.205V to be no more than an interim variant of the C.202, and he soon focused on an even more refined version of his fighter. To make full use of the new DB 605A-1 engine, Castoldi modified the airframe to produce the C.205N *Orione* (Orion). For the first time, the C.202/205's wingspan was increased from 34ft 8.5in to 36ft 10.85in. The tail surfaces of the new machine were identical to those of the *Veltro*, but the fuselage ratio was refined and the wing machine guns/cannons were removed. Armed with four 12.7mm machine guns (grouped in the forward fuselage) and one engine-mounted Mauser MG 151 20mm cannon, the prototype C.205N-1 (MM499) finally addressed the armament issues that had afflicted previous Italian fighters. The first prototype took to the air on 1 November 1942, and it was followed by a second machine that was even more heavily armed – the C.205N-2 was fitted with three 20mm cannon and two 12.7mm machine guns.

Although packing a greater punch than the *Veltro*, the C.205N was actually slower (maximum speed of 390mph at 22,965ft) than its predecessor. And Macchi would have had to create new tooling in order to mass-produce the *Orione*. Unsurprisingly, the C.205N was not put into production. Development did continue with the C.206 and C.207 variants, however, both of which would use a similar engine and airframe combination to that fitted in the *Orione*, but married to a new wing of 40ft 9in – into which four Mauser MG 151 20mm cannon had been installed. Two prototypes were under construction at the time of the Italian armistice.

The last of Dr Mario Castoldi's long line of Macchi fighters was the C.202V *Veltro*, which remained in limited production into 1945. Many were supplied to the Germans and units of the ANR fighting in northern Italy alongside the Luftwaffe. One variant that did not make it into production, however, was the C.205N-1 *Orione*, the prototype of which (MM499) is seen here. This aircraft was one of just two examples built, being flown for the first time on 1 November 1942. The *Orione* had a greater wingspan than the C.202/205 and improved armament (four 12.7mm machine guns and a single 20mm cannon). (Author)

Able to use existing *Folgore* production jigs and tools, Macchi gave priority to the C.205V. In the end, only 177 had been delivered prior to the armistice coming into force, with a further 112 being delivered to the fascist *Aeronautica Nazionle Repubblicana* (ANR) before the Macchi factory was destroyed by Allied heavy bombers in May 1944.

Other Italian fighter designers would harness the power of the DB 601/605 series of engines with great results. Fiat would produce the superlative Fiat G.55 *Centauro* (Centaur), which was powered by the DB 605A-1 or licence-built *Tifone*. Capable of a top speed of 385mph at 22,965ft, the fighter was armed with one Mauser MG 151 20mm cannon and four Breda-SAFAT 12.7mm machine guns. Just 31 G.55s had been built by the time the armistice came into affect, although an additional 164 were completed for the ANR before the Fiat factory was heavily bombed by the Allies in April 1944.

Reggiane would also produce a DB 605-powered fighter as a follow-on to the Re.2001. The more streamlined, and aptly named, Re.2005 *Sagittario* (Archer) incorporated the same wing as fitted to earlier Reggiane fighters, but its fuselage was extensively redesigned and the resulting airframe mated to a DB 605A-1 or *Tifone* engine. Armament consisted of one engine-mounted Mauser MG 151 20mm cannon and two Breda-SAFAT 12.7 mm machine guns in the wings. The fighter's top speed was an impressive 390mph at 22,800ft. Just 32 examples were built.

Italy's poor industrial base led directly the C.202's failure in combat. Forced to rely on Germany for raw materials, and suffering the continual loss of skilled workers, the Italian aircraft industry had little hope of keeping pace with wartime demands. Had the C.202 been built in adequate numbers with better armament, and supplied to units along with enough fuel, sufficient spare parts and properly trained pilots, the outcome of the air war in the Mediterranean could have been very different.

TECHNICAL
SPECIFICATIONS

SPITFIRE

PROTOTYPE SPITFIRE K5054

The first Spitfire ever built filled two roles. Between 5 March 1936 and delivery of the first Spitfire I in May 1938, the aircraft served as both a prototype and a pre-production development machine. Hand-built, K5054 was originally powered by a 990hp Merlin 'C' (Merlin II) and soon reached a top speed of 349.5mph. Progressive testing by both Supermarine and the RAF saw the fitting of more powerful engines, including the Merlin 'F' (1,035hp) and the Merlin II (1,030hp). Standard armament was eight 0.303-in. Browning machine guns, with four in each wing and 300 rounds per weapon. By late October 1938, 20 production-standard Spitfire Is were in the process of work-up trials with the RAF. On 4 September 1939, after serving as a high-speed hack at Farnborough, K5054 suffered a landing accident and was written off.

SPITFIRE I

In April 1938 production of the Spitfire I began. Entering service with No. 19 Sqn on 4 August 1938, the Spitfire I was fitted with a two-bladed, fixed-pitch Watts wooden propeller. Early production Mk Is were powered by the Merlin II engine. After the

The Spitfire VA was virtually indistinguishable from the Mk I and II. Equipped with the A-type wing, it featured the same exhaust stubs, canopy and de Havilland propeller as fitted to the early marks. In fact the only way to identify a Mk VA from a Spitfire I or II was by the larger oil cooler, with its deeper housing and circular air intake, located under the port wing. This aircraft is R7347, which was one of two early build Mk VAs sent to Wright Field in Dayton, Ohio, in May 1941 for evaluation by the US Army Air Corps. (Author)

64th example had been built Supermarine switched to the Merlin III engine combined with a more efficient three-bladed de Havilland or Rotol two-pitch or constant speed propeller. Speed was duly increased and the take-off run reduced by up to 400 yards. Armour was also added, with a 75lb plate installed behind the pilot and a thick laminated pane of bulletproof glass fitted to the windscreen. Production of the Mk I totalled 1,567 aircraft.

SPITFIRE IA/IB

All Spitfires equipped with eight 0.303-in. Browning machine guns were designated as IAs in the summer of 1940. This was done to differentiate them from the new cannon-armed Spitfires, a small number of which had been fitted with two 20mm Hispano-Suiza Type 404 cannon and issued exclusively to No. 19 Sqn during the Battle of Britain. Designated as Mk IBs, these aircraft suffered from chronic jamming problems in combat and were quickly withdrawn from service.

SPITFIRE IIA/B

Built in the massive Shadow Factory established by the Nuffield Organisation in Castle Bromwich, these aircraft were fitted with the slightly more powerful Merlin XII engine. Production ended in July 1941, with 751 Mk IIAs (armed with eight 0.303-in. machine guns) and 170 Mk IIBs (fitted with 20mm cannon) being built.

SPITFIRE III

Originally intended to replace the Mks I and II in production, the Spitfire III had a re-engineered and strengthened airframe and was powered by the new Merlin XX engine that featured a redesigned supercharger and two separate blowers. The Merlin XX proved to be a complicated engine to build in sufficient numbers, so priority then switched to the Spitfire V, fitted with a simplified version of the Merlin XX known as the Merlin 45. Only one Spitfire III (N3297) was built.

SPITFIRE IV

Development of the Mk IV proceeded in parallel with the Spitfire III. This version was powered by the new Rolls-Royce Griffon IIB engine developing 1,490hp at 14,000ft. One prototype (DP845) was built, and the aircraft made its maiden flight from Worthy Down on 27 November 1941. The Spitfire IV would go on to serve as the prototype for the Griffon-engined Spitfire XII.

SPITFIRE V

The Spitfire V was simply a Mk I airframe fitted with the new Merlin 45, 46, 50 or 50A engine. The Merlin 45 was the less complicated version of the Merlin XX, which powered the Mk III. The supercharger's second stage was removed and a new single-speed single stage supercharger fitted in its place. The Merlin 45 was rated at 1,440hp on takeoff and was easy to mass produce. Other improvements incorporated into the engine included a new carburettor, which allowed for negative G manoeuvres and no interruption of fuel flow to the engine. Pilots soon found the Merlin 45-powered Spitfire V ran at excessively high oil temperatures. The original engine cooling system of the Spitfire I was not powerful enough, so a larger matrix had to be fitted to the cooler, which in turn required a larger air intake – the new oil cooler intake was enlarged and made circular in shape. The Spitfire I's fabric ailerons were also replaced with examples made from light alloy.

The first Spitfire Vs built were fitted with the A–type wing which housed eight 0.303-in. Browning machine guns. Armour plating was also increased, weighing in at 129lb. Top speed for the Spitfire VA was 375mph at 20,800ft, and just 94 were built.

The Spitfire VB would ultimately be the most-produced Mk V variant. It featured the B-type wing, which housed two Hispano 20mm cannon, with 60 rounds per weapon, and four 0.303–in. Browning machine guns with 350 rounds per gun. Armour was increased in weight to 152lb.

The initial production versions of the Spitfire VA and VB were merely Mk Is and IIs fitted with a Merlin 45 engine. The Mk VC (production of which began in October 1941) featured a redesigned and strengthened airframe. It was also fitted with the C-type or 'universal' wing and a short spinner. Very few photographs exist of a Mk VC without a Vokes filter, as seen here, before production switched to the tropical version. (Author)

Spitfire VA AB320 was converted into a Mk VB and used as the prototype for the first fully tropicalized Mk V. The most visible modification was the addition of the prominent Vokes filter beneath the nose. A tropical radiator and oil cooler were installed, and the aircraft also had provision for an external slipper tank of 90 gallons. Other internal changes included the addition of tropical survival gear, which consisted of a 1.5 gallon tank filled with drinking water and a container for flying rations, a signal pistol and cartridges, an emergency tool roll and a heliograph mirror and ground signalling strips. Air tests revealed that the Spitfire VB Trop fitted with a Merlin 45 engine had a top speed of 337.5mph at 17,400ft. Rate-of-climb was 2,145ft per minute, with a ceiling of 34,500ft.

A total of 3,911 Spitfire VBs would be built, 776 by Supermarine, 2,995 in Castle Bromwich and 140 by Westland.

The Spitfire VC introduced the 'universal' C-type wing that was first tested on the Spitfire III prototype. This variant also featured all of the tropical modifications found on the VB Trop. The 'universal wing' was designed to reduce manufacturing time and allowed for three different armament options. The 'C' wing featured either eight 0.303-in. machine guns, two 20mm cannon and four 0.303-in. machine guns or four 20mm cannon. The Hispano Mk II cannon were now belt fed from box magazines, thus doubling the ammunition per weapon to 120 rounds. Early build Spitfire VCs were delivered with four 20mm cannon, but two of these weapons were usually removed once the fighter was in frontline service. Later, production would shift back to the B-type wing of two 20mm cannon and four 0.303-in. machine guns.

The airframe of the Spitfire VC was also re-stressed and strengthened, and it introduced the new laminated windscreen design as seen on the Mk III. Metal ailerons

Operation *Bowery*, on 9 May 1942, would see 64 Spitfire VC Trops take off from *Wasp* and *Eagle* and fly 600+ miles due east to Malta. In order to reach their destination, each Mk VC Trop was equipped with a 90-gallon slipper tank – the one fitted to this particular aircraft aboard *Wasp* has been clearly marked with the word *GASSED* in white chalk to denote to deck crew that the fighter is ready for take off. With the large but vital Vokes filter, full armament of four 20mm cannon and eight 0.303-in. machine guns and a 90-gallon slipper tank, the Mk VC Trop, as seen here, would be the heaviest Merlin-engined Spitfire variant to take off from an aircraft carrier during World War II. The concentration on the pilot's face is clearly evident as US Navy deckcrewmen hold back the Spitfire just moments before its very short, and potentially dangerous, take-off run. (Author)

SPITFIRE VC WING GUNS

The first Spitfire VCs delivered to Malta were the most heavily armed Supermarine fighters of the war, featuring four Hispano Mk II 20mm cannon. Persistent stoppages due to faulty ammunition soon forced RAF armourers on Malta to remove two of the 20mm cannon, however. Spitfire armament on the island varied throughout the campaign, and it was not uncommon for aircraft to be fitted with just two 20mm cannon and two Browning 0.303-in. machine guns as seen here. Both the Hispanos and the Brownings drew their ammunition from separate magazines within the wings, there being 120 rounds per gun for the cannon and 350 rounds per weapon for the machine guns.

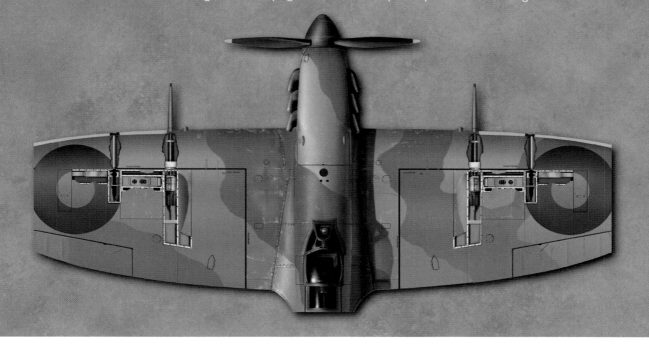

were introduced, along with a stiffened undercarriage with wheels that had been moved two inches forward. Armour was increased to 193lb.

To increase the Spitfire VC's ferry range a 29-gallon fuel tank was installed behind the pilot. This, combined with a 90-gallon slipper tank, meant that the Mk VC could carry up to 204 gallons of fuel which gave it a ferry range of approximately 700 miles. When fitted with four 20mm cannon, the Spitfire VC had a top speed of 374mph at 19,000ft. The Mk VC served mainly in overseas theatres, including the Middle East, Burma and Australia. Some 2,467 Spitfire VCs would be built, 478 by Supermarine, 1,494 in Castle Bromwich and 495 by Westland.

In order to improve the low-level performance of the Spitfire V, a number of Mk VB airframes were modified and fitted with either the Merlin 45M, 50M or 55M powerplant. The 'M' suffix denoted a Merlin engine equipped with a cropped supercharger blower that worked best at lower altitudes – indeed the motor gave its optimum performance at 6,000ft. The airframe was also modified, with the Spitfire's famous pointed wingtips being removed to reduce the wingspan to 32ft 6in. The new square-tipped wings gave the LF (Low Altitude Fighter) V a greater diving speed, better acceleration and faster rate-of-roll when compared to a standard Spitfire V.

Many LF Vs used Mk VB airframes taken from storage and duly modified. Due to the aircrafts' previous service, the LF Vs were soon nicknamed 'the clipped, cropped and clapped Spittys'. At low altitude the LF V had a maximum speed of 338.5mph at 2,000ft and 355.5mph at 5,900ft.

The Mk V version of the famous Spitfire would be built in greater numbers than any other variant. It would be powered by nine different types of Merlin 45 engine and would see action on every front. The Mk V would also be navalized and transformed into the Seafire IB, IIC and III. The carrier-borne version of the Spitfire would take the fight to the enemy over the Atlantic, Indian and Pacific Oceans and the Mediterranean Sea.

A close up of the starboard Breda-SAFAT 12.7mm machine gun. The weapon weighed 64lb and had a muzzle velocity of 2,510ft per second. Surprisingly, some pilots like Capt Furio Doglio Niclot would swap out one of these weapons for a 7mm gun in order to lighten their aircraft and improve its performance. With a C.202 in this configuration, the only chance a pilot had of achieving a kill was to fire a burst from point blank range. (Author)

C.202 *FOLGORE*

C.200 *SAETTA*

The C.200 was an all-metal cantilever low-wing monoplane with hydraulically retractable landing gear and a fully enclosed cockpit (early in the production run this was changed to an open and then a partially enclosed cockpit). Its Fiat A 74 RC38 14-cylinder two-row geared and supercharged air-cooled radial engine developed 870hp at take off and gave the fighter a top speed of 312mph at 14,750ft. The C.200 was equipped with two Breda-SAFAT 12.7mm machine guns (with 370 rounds per weapon) mounted in front of the pilot. Total production reached 1,153 aircraft.

PROTOTYPE C.202 MM445

The C.202 prototype retained many of the C.200's components, including its landing gear, vertical tail and tailplanes, the two 12.7mm machine guns and the asymmetrical wing, with the port wing being 7.87in longer (this was done to compensate for propeller torque). They were mated to an all-new fuselage, with the most noticeable modification being the lowering of the upper fuselage decking. The aircraft employed an all-metal flush riveted structure, with a semi-monocoque oval-section fuselage and a three-piece two-spar wing. The fuselage was covered with 'avional duralumin' and housed two self-sealing fuel tanks. The ailerons, rudder and elevators were fabric covered. Powered by a DB 601A-1 engine developing 1,175hp, the prototype first flew on 10 August 1940. Test flights at the *Centro Sperimentale* confirmed the soundness of the new fighter, which recorded a top speed of 370mph at 18,730ft and took just 6 min 13 sec to reach 19,700ft. Only one prototype was built.

C.202 *FOLGORE*

The first production C.202s differed only slightly from the original prototype. The supercharger air intake was extended, the glazed panelling aft of the pilot's seat was removed and the aft deck was scalloped to improve the pilot's rearward view. The retractable tailwheel was replaced by a semi-fared unit. Power was provided by the RA 1000 RC41-I *Monsone* engine driving a 9ft 10.333in diameter constant-speed three-bladed Piaggio P.1001 metal airscrew. Armament consisted of two synchronized Breda-SAFAT 12.7mm machine guns, with 400 rounds per gun. Takeoff weight reached 6,206lb. Comparative trials between a fully equipped production *Folgore* and the prototype showed that the latter was only fractionally faster.

Folgores equipped with a dust filter over the supercharger air intake were given the suffix AS (*Africa Settentrionale*). Virtually all *Folgores* produced were equipped with the AS filter.

The C.202CB (*Caccia Bombardiere*) was the fighter-bomber version of the *Folgore*. Beginning with Breda-built Serie VII aircraft, armament consisted of two nose-mounted Breda-SAFAT 12.7mm machine guns and a single 7.7mm machine gun in each wing (the latter with 500 rounds per gun). Bomb racks were installed (along with wing plumbing) to permit the fitment of two drop tanks of up to 33 imperial gallons or two 353lb bombs. A small number of *Folgores* were also built as reconnaissance fighters, given the suffix RF. These aircraft were fitted with vertical cameras in place of the radio set.

Due to the C.202's very short production run (1941–43), the number of modifications made to the aircraft during that time were minor, and they had no overall affect on its performance. Indeed, the only major change was the increase in armament introduced with the Macchi-built Serie VII (MM9025 to MM9124).

To meet demand for the new fighter, production was shared between three companies – Macchi, Breda and SAI-Ambrosini. Early build C.202s were fitted with DB 601A-1 engines supplied directly by Daimler-Benz. Later variants were fitted with licence-built RA 1000 RC41-I engines. The number of C.202s built was extremely small – 1,150. This was due to the anaemic production rate of the RA 1000, which totalled just 60 engines per month. The C.202 was built in 13 production series. Three more were planned but never built. The listing that follows identifies the individual production series and the modifications made in each.

SERIE I

One hundred aircraft were built at the Breda factory between July 1941 and March 1942 (serial nos MM7859 to MM7958). These aircraft differed from the prototype through the fitment of a long air intake for the supercharger, but they lacked dust filters. The rear cockpit glazing was replaced with a metal sheet. The retractable tailwheel was replaced with a fixed unit and the welded engine mount was replaced with a forged one.

The clean and compact engine installation of the DB 601 in the C.202 gave the fighter a very small frontal area, just as it did in the Bf 109. The forged magnesium alloy cantilever engine mounting was also very similar to the one used in the Messerschmitt fighter. (Author)

A close up of the tail unit of Sergente Maggiore Faliero Gelli's crash-landed C.202 of 378ª *Squadriglia*, 155° *Gruppo*, 51° *Stormo*. He was Flt Sgt George Beurling's 13th victim, shot down on 27 July 1942. This aircraft was a Serie III built by Macchi between May 1941 and April 1942. The *Regia Aeronautica's* 'Stemma Sabaudo' coat of arms of Italy emblem can be clearly seen in the centre of the white cross on the rudder. (Author)

SERIE II

Identical to the Serie I machines, these aircraft (MM7709 to MM7718) were the first ten production C.202s built by Macchi in April–May 1941.

SERIE III

Serie III consisted of 140 C.202s built by Macchi from May 1941 through to April 1942 (MM7719 to MM7858). These aircraft introduced changes necessary for desert conditions, including a dust filter fitted to the supercharger air intake. These aircraft were designated C.202AS. A larger oil cooler, cooling vents in the machine gun covers and a cockpit air intake were also added.

SERIE IV

These aircraft were built by SAI-Ambrosini, the 50 (MM7409 to MM7458) in Serie IV featuring similar changes to the late Serie III *Folgores*.

SERIE V

Fifty machines were constructed by SAI-Ambrosini (MM7959 to MM8008) between May 1941 and July 1942. Early examples were similar to the Serie IV aircraft, while late-build examples had modifications similar to the Serie VII. A more modern San Giorgio C reflector gunsight was also fitted.

SERIE VI

Fifty aircraft (MM8081 to MM8130) were built by Breda in the spring of 1942.

SERIE VII

One hundred C.202s (MM9023 to MM9122) were constructed by Macchi between April and July 1942. This Serie saw the introduction of a Breda-SAFAT 7.7mm machine gun in each wing (500 rounds per gun). This did little to increase overall firepower, but it did increase the take-off weight from 6,460lb to 6,766lb. The added weight adversely affected the aircraft's performance, and the wing guns were often removed in the field. Serie VII machines were fitted with two bomb racks and plumbing for drop tanks. Other modifications included a central armoured glass panel and additional armour plating aft of the pilot's seat. From mid-1942 a new 'D' type tailwheel was also fitted. At the same time production of the RA 1000 RC41-I at last reached levels sufficient for the C.202 to be fitted with the new engine, rather than an imported DB 601A-1.

SERIE VIII

Fifty Breda-manufactured C.202s (MM8339 to MM8388) were built between March and July 1942.

C.202 *FOLGORE* COWLING AND WING GUNS

Boasting just two Breda-SAFAT 12.7mm and two 7.7mm machine guns, the C.202 was one of the most lightly armed single-seat fighters of World War II. It was further handicapped by having the engine-mounted guns synchronized to fire through the propeller arc. This reduced the rate-of-fire by up to 30 per cent depending on engine rpm. The 12.7mm guns held 400 rounds per gun, while 7.7mm weapons were equipped with 500 rounds per gun for approximately 34 seconds of firing.

SERIE IX

One hundred machines built by Macchi (MM9389 to MM9490) came off the assembly lines from September 1941 through to February 1942.

SERIE X

One hundred aircraft were produced by the Breda factory (MM9500 to MM9601) between July and September 1942.

SERIE XI

Some 150 aircraft were built by Breda from November 1942 through to April 1943 (MM9602 to MM9753). Minor modifications to late Serie XI aircraft included a new horizontal tail and the relocation of the venturi from the underside of the fuselage to the starboard side of the aircraft beneath the cockpit.

SERIE XII

These aircraft were similar to the C.202 Serie XI (late) machines and were assembled under German control at the Breda factory between May and August 1943 – 150 aircraft were built (MM9803 to MM9952).

SERIE XIII

These were the last production Serie C.202s built during the war, with 50 aircraft being produced by Macchi (MM9953 to MM10002) from April through to August 1943. They incorporated the same modifications made to Serie XI (late) machines.

A VIEW FROM THE COCKPIT

In the summer of 1943 British Air Intelligence got to examine a C.202 up close for the first time when one was captured intact, but not airworthy, in Libya. Serie III aircraft MM7779 of 96ª *Squadriglia*, 9° *Gruppo*, 4° *Stormo* was powered by an imported DB 601A-1 engine. Enemy Aircraft Report No. 48/1 provides a good description of the cockpit:

The view from the cockpit is fair in all directions. The front three transparent panels are of triplex glass and the remainder of a material of the Perspex type. No rearview mirror is fitted. The hood can be opened from either side by a separate release handle on each side or jettisoned by using both handles at once. The front panel of each of the side windows can be slid back if required.

The cockpit is comfortable and fairly roomy and has plenty of headroom. Neither the seat nor rudder bar are adjustable.

The pilot is well protected by armour plate from astern and, in fact, to about 40 degrees off dead astern. He is provided with a bucket seat entirely constructed from a single piece of 8mm armour, which stretches from his shoulders almost to his knees and comes well round the sides of his body. The armour plate seat appears to be hand made. In addition there is a headpiece of 7mm armour and a small strip to cover the gap between the two. No bulletproof glass is used on this aeroplane.

The only armament on this aeroplane comprises two machine guns mounted in front of the pilot firing over the engine and through the airscrew disc. The guns are mechanically synchronized with the propeller. The guns are mechanically cocked by two T-handles in the cockpit and are probably electrically fired by a button, which was missing, on the control column. Round counters are provided on the lower instrument panel for each of the guns. The counters read up to 650 rounds per gun and show a red warning mark when the number of rounds is reduced to 75 per gun.

The cockpit fittings on the whole are inferior and the layout has none of the neatness of German cockpits.

Spitfire VC Trop and C.202 Comparison Specifications		
	Spitfire VC Trop	**C.202**
Powerplant	1,470hp Rolls-Royce Merlin 45	1,175 Daimler-Benz DB 601A-1
Dimensions		
Span	36ft 10in	34ft 8in
Length	29ft 11in	29ft 0.5in
Height	12ft 7.75in	9ft 11.5in
Wing area	242 sq. ft	180.84 sq. ft
Weights		
Empty	5,100lb	5,545lb
Loaded	6,785lb	6,766lb
Performance		
Max speed	354mph at 17,400ft	372mph at 18,370ft
Range	470 miles	475 miles
Climb	to 20,000ft in 8 min	to 19,685ft in 5.55 min
Service Ceiling	36,300ft	37,730ft
Armament	4 x 20mm Hispano cannon or 2 x 20mm Hispano cannon and 4 x 0.303-in. Brownings	2 x 12.7mm and 2 x 7.7mm Breda-SAFAT machine guns

THE STRATEGIC SITUATION

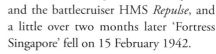

After nearly two-and-half years of war Britain was still very much on the back foot in the spring of 1942. The British Army had yet to claim a single victory of note against the *Wehrmacht*, with defeats and setbacks being experienced in almost every theatre, from northern Europe to North Africa and the Far East. In the latter theatre British and Commonwealth forces would experience a series of humiliating reversals. On 10 December 1941 Japanese torpedo-bombers sank the battleship HMS *Prince of Wales* and the battlecruiser HMS *Repulse*, and a little over two months later 'Fortress Singapore' fell on 15 February 1942.

Three days earlier both the RAF and Royal Navy had suffered another dispiriting defeat when, under cover of darkness, the pride of the *Kriegsmarine* – the battlecruisers *Scharnhorst* and *Gneisenau*, and the heavy cruiser *Prince Eugen* – sailed from Brest harbour, through the English Channel and back to German waters. The best the British could muster to oppose them were six Swordfish biplane torpedo-bombers, all of which were shot down attempting to attack the vessels.

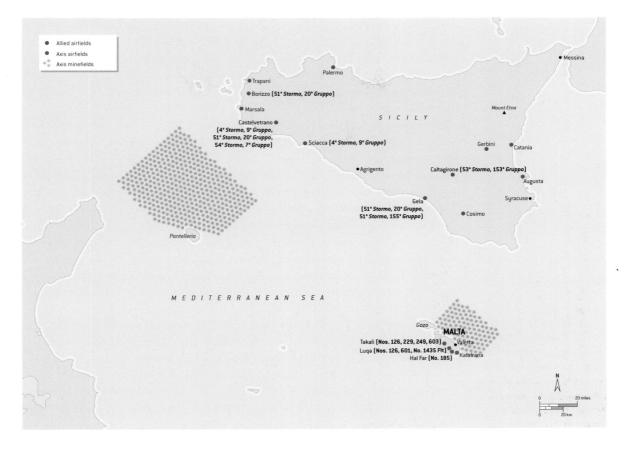

Allied airfields
Axis airfields
Axis minefields

Messina

Trapani
Palermo
Borizzo [51° Stormo, 20° Gruppo]
Marsala
Castelvetrano ●
[4° Stormo, 9° Gruppo,
51° Stormo, 20° Gruppo,
54° Stormo, 7° Gruppo]

S I C I L Y

Mount Etna

Sciacca [4° Stormo, 9° Gruppo]
Gerbini
Catania
Agrigento
Caltagirone [53° Stormo, 153° Gruppo]
Augusta
Gela
[51° Stormo, 20° Gruppo,
51° Stormo, 155° Gruppo]
Cosimo
Syracuse

Pantelleria

M E D I T E R R A N E A N   S E A

Gozo
MALTA
Takali [Nos. 126, 229, 249, 603] ●
Valetta
Luqa [Nos. 126, 601, No. 1435 Flt] ●
Hal Far [No. 185]
Kalafrana

N

0   20 miles
0   20 km

C.202 and Spitfire V unit dispositions on Sicily and Malta between March and October 1942.

The RAF for its part had suffered four resounding defeats – the aerial campaign in Norway and the battles of France, Greece and Malaya. The only victory had been the Battle of Britain, which, although often described as being a 'decisive' triumph over the Luftwaffe, was in fact a battle won by a combination of a robust and sophisticated British defence matched by a flawed German tactical and strategic plan. While the RAF shot down a large number of German aircraft, the Luftwaffe's inability to neutralise RAF airfields and the decision to switch its attacks to the city of London in September 1940 played into British hands and effectively gave them the tactical advantage.

By the spring of 1942 the island of Malta, in the Mediterranean, had been under siege for almost two years. Described by Winston Churchill as 'the master key to the British Empire', Malta would prove to be a decisive strategic asset. Despite its small size, Malta was a vital link for the sea routes between Gibraltar, North Africa and the Middle East. For the Axis powers Malta would prove a serious threat to all shipping heading for North Africa from Italy. Indeed, British submarines, destroyers and aircraft operating from Malta had been highly effective in disrupting the flow of supplies in the first two years of the conflict, sinking or damaging more than half-a-million tons of Axis shipping.

The siege of Malta began shortly after Italy entered the war against Britain and France. On the morning of 11 June 1940, 33 Savoia-Marchetti SM.79 bombers, escorted by 18 CR.42 biplane fighters, attacked Valetta harbour. Fortunately for the Italians, British air defences at the time consisted of just four Fleet Air Arm Gloster Gladiator biplane fighters. It was a token force, and one the *Regia Aeronautica* should have easily destroyed. However, the subsequent struggle that the Italians had trying to neutralize the makeshift aerial defence of the island starkly reveals how unprepared the *Regia Aeronautica* was for war. It was a second rate force, both technically and numerically.

When Italy declared war on the Allies on 10 June 1940, the *Regia Aeronautica's* total strength consisted of 3,269 aircraft, of which only 1,795 were considered combat ready. The frontline force could field just 542 fighters – 77 C.200s, 88 G.50s, 200 CR.42s and 177 CR.32s. A further 165 fighters were not combat ready while 287 more were either being repaired or undergoing routine servicing. It was not a firm base on which to begin offensive operations. The *Regia Aeronautica* had hoped for a short series of campaigns that would gain its units early victories and not stretch its limited resources. While morale was high at the beginning of the war, Mussolini's ill-fated decisions would force the *Regia Aeronautica* to fight on far too many fronts with too few aircraft. Indeed, sustained air operations against British and French military targets in the greater Mediterranean and Middle East were limited by the range of Italian medium bombers and their small bomb load.

The attack on Malta that began on 11 June 1940 would continue for three months without result. On 21 June eight Hurricanes had been hurriedly flown in via France, and they would provide the RAF with enough of a defence to keep the *Regia Aeronautica* at bay. Between September and December Italian forces would be committed to the invasion of Greece and a desert offensive against the British in North Africa. A contingent of 178 fighters and bombers was also sent to Belgium to belatedly join the Luftwaffe in the Battle of Britain. None of these operations brought the Italians any success. In fact they led directly to German intervention in the Balkans and North Africa.

On 9 December 1940 the mechanized Western Desert Force (consisting of troops from the Indian 4th Division and tanks from the British 7th Armoured Division) launched Operation *Compass* to counterattack the Italian offensive of 9 September. Mussolini had ordered the latter in the hope that it would expand Italian influence in the Mediterranean by linking Italian North Africa with Italian East Africa, capturing the Suez Canal and the Arabian oilfields in the process. Italian troops were caught completely off-guard, and by 10 December the British and Indian forces had taken more than 20,000 prisoners. When this offensive was halted by Prime Minister Winston Churchill on 9 February 1941, no fewer than 130,000 Italians had been captured, along with 200 artillery pieces, 100 tanks and 1,500 vehicles. The *Regia Aeronautica* had also suffered heavy losses during *Compass*, with nearly 700 aircraft being destroyed in total.

This Luftwaffe attack map from 3 April 1942 shows the targets and units involved in the day and night attacks on Malta on that date, as well as the direction from which they approached their targets. The units participating included fighters from I./JG 53 (*Jabos*), nightfighters from 4./NJG 2 and bombers from I./KG 54, III./KG 77 and KGr. 806. Malta suffered three major raids on the 3rd, and they mostly went unchallenged due to the poor state of serviceability amongst the defending RAF fighters. (Author)

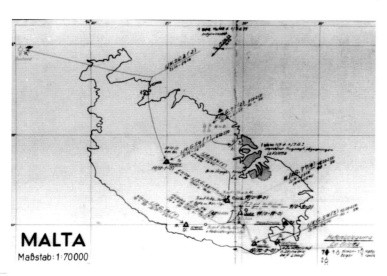

MALTA

Maßstab: 1:70000

To help save the Italian army from complete collapse Hitler ordered Generalleutnant Erwin Rommel to North Africa. On 11 February 1941 elements of the *Deutsches Afrika Korps* began to arrive in Libya.

With the Germans firmly entrenched in North Africa by the spring of 1941, the strategic importance of Malta came to the fore. Exasperated by the failure of the *Regia Aeronautica* to eliminate both the offensive and defensive capabilities of the RAF on Malta, the Luftwaffe entered the fray with the arrival of X. *Fliegerkorps* on Sicily in early 1941. Initially, the German aerial strength consisted of units flying 80 Ju 88A-4s, 50 He 111H-6s, 80 Ju 87R-1s and an undisclosed number of Bf 110C-4s. In February 14 Bf 109E-7s joined the fight. The *Regia Aeronautica* committed 45 SM.79 bombers and 75 CR.42 and C.200 fighters to the order of battle.

In the defence of Malta the British could muster just six Hurricane IIs, four Fairey Fulmar Is and a solitary Sea Gladiator. It was a one-sided fight, and by late February 1941 Axis forces were in control of the skies over the central Mediterranean. This in turn stopped all supply convoys to Malta. If there had been a perfect time for the Axis forces to invade the island this would have been it. Across the Mediterranean British forces were suffering a series of defeats. In the desert the newly arrived *Afrika Korps* launched a counteroffensive that drove British troops back into Egypt. In the Balkans German ground and air units invaded Yugoslavia, Greece and Crete. X. *Fliegerkorps* was then shifted from Sicily to bases in Greece, Crete and Rhodes.

This proved to be a major tactical blunder, however, for the focus of attention was temporarily moved off Malta. Making the most of this break in the action, the RAF flew 35 Hurricane IIAs off the flightdeck of HMS *Ark Royal* and into Malta in April.

A short while later the *Regia Aeronautica* commenced a new campaign against Malta. In May 7° *Gruppo* transferred to Ciampino, followed by 16° *Gruppo* in June.

Spitfires had been trickling into Malta since 7 March 1942, with the first 31 being delivered by the carrier HMS *Eagle* during three trips that month. This was not enough, however, as attrition quickly reduced their numbers. Following its third delivery run on 29 March *Eagle* was forced to remain in Gibraltar Harbour for much of April undergoing repairs to its damaged steering gear. With no British carriers available, Prime Minister Winston Churchill secured US assistance in the form of the 19,000-ton carrier *Wasp*. In Operation *Calendar* on 20 April 1942, 46 Spitfire VCs were successfully launched from the vessel. Here, the pilot of Spitfire VC Trop BR185/2-R, assigned to No. 603 Sqn, runs up his engine prior to take off. BR185 was subsequently damaged beyond repair on 3 May 1942. (Author)

Pilots of the Takali Wing pose for the camera in August 1942. They are, from left to right, Sgt Stan Shewell, Plt Offs Vincent 'Junior' Moody and George Beurling, Flt Lt George Swannick, Wg Cdr Arthur Donaldson, Plt Off Frank Johnson and Sqn Ldr Bill Douglas. (Author)

On 22 June 1941 Hitler put into action his ambitious plan to invade the USSR. Operation *Barbarossa* was the largest military offensive in modern history, and it would have a direct impact on the fate of Malta. Just prior to its launching, German air assets were transferred directly to the Eastern Front, leaving the *Regia Aeronautica* with the task of keeping Malta in check. However, as the island's defences grew (a further 43 Hurricane IIs arrived in June 1941), so too did its offensive capabilities. Between June and September Malta-based ships, submarines and aircraft sank 270,000 tons of enemy shipping. In October and November things got worse, with 20 per cent of all supplies sent from Italy to North Africa being lost.

Rommel could no longer tolerate this situation, and in the autumn of 1941 he pressed for additional air power to neutralize Malta once and for all. At the same time the C.202 would make its combat debut over Malta. In October 4° *Stormo's* 9° *Gruppo* replaced its old C.200s with brand new C.202s and began operations over Malta. Unfortunately for the British the arrival of winter on the Eastern Front also meant that the Luftwaffe could transfer II. *Fliegerkorps* to Sicily. During December 1941 and January 1942 its units began trickling into airfields on Sicily. The slow force build up meant that full-scale operations could not begin until March, however.

The arrival of Luftwaffe units in Sicily also saw the relocation of some *Regia Aeronautica* squadrons, which joined the substantial force already in place on the island. At full strength II. *Fliegerkorps* had in excess of 400 aircraft, with the *Regia Aeronautica* contributing 50 bombers/torpedo-bombers, about 100 fighters and 60 rescue/reconnaissance aircraft. In defence the RAF had of a mix of Hurricane IIBs and Cs spread between three squadrons, two partial squadrons and one flight.

The German/Italian plan of attack was to first destroy all British aircraft, in the air and on the ground, knock out the island's radar system, blockade its ports and runways against all resupply attempts, mine the approaches to all harbours and destroy their installations.

Clearly outclassed by the Bf 109F-4 and newly arrived C.202s, the RAF knew that the only hope it had of defending Malta lay with the Spitfire V. On 7 March 1942, flying off the carrier HMS *Eagle*, the first 15 Spitfire Vs were delivered to Malta. In the weeks and months that followed more Spitfires would be delivered.

For the first three months of 1942 the attacks on Malta had been essentially a Luftwaffe preserve by day, but this was about to change. At sunset on 2 April 4° *Stormo* flew in to Sicily with 26 new C.202s. For the next seven months Italy's best fighter would be pitted against the formidable Spitfire V. It would be a battle in which only the best aircraft, and pilots, would survive.

THE COMBATANTS

At the outbreak of war RAF Fighter Command was able to muster 39 squadrons of fighters – 30 squadrons of single-seat fighters comprising 570 Hurricanes, Spitfires, Defiants and Gladiators, with 659 pilots, seven squadrons equipped with twin-engined Blenheim Is and two squadrons flying obsolete Gauntlet and Hind biplane fighters.

During the Battle of Britain the rapid loss of seasoned pilots forced Training Command to cut corners. By drawing pilots from Coastal and Bomber Commands, as well as the Fleet Air Arm and Army Cooperation squadrons, and drastically cutting some training courses from months to just weeks, Fighter Command was able to keep its units operational. Towards the end of 1940 the pilot crisis began to ease, and by December 1941 Fighter Command could boast 60 squadrons of Spitfires alone (the majority equipped with Mk VBs). There were also units flying Hurricanes, as well as Mosquito and Beaufighter nightfighters. The rapid increase in the size of Fighter Command had been a tremendous feat of arms. This had been achieved through the establishment of the British Commonwealth Air Training Plan (BCATP) in North America, southern Africa and Australia from mid-1941, which allowed pilots to be trained by the hundreds. After the Battle of Britain, RAF Fighter Command would never again suffer from a lack of well-trained pilots.

By comparison, the number of new pilots available to the *Regia Aeronautica* failed to increase as the war progressed. And despite the victorious campaigns in Ethiopia (1934–36) and during the Spanish Civil War (1936–39), the *Regia Aeronautica* was not ready for combat when Italy declared war on the Allies in June 1940.

Unfortunately for the Italians, the lessons learned during the Spanish Civil War would not serve them well. Aircraft losses (188 to all causes) and aircrew attrition (200) depleted its frontline strength and slowed aircraft development. More importantly, both factors impeded pilot training. Italian fighters (CR.32s) had flown

Flt Lt Henry Wallace McLeod joined the RCAF at the start of September 1940 and subsequently graduated from the rapidly expanding British Commonwealth Air Training Plan early the following year. Reaching the UK in May 1941 with the rank of pilot officer, he flew to Malta with 25 other Spitfire pilots as part of Operation *Style* on 3 June 1942. He would run up a score of 13 victories, three of which were C. 202s, making him second to Beurling's six C.202 victories. Later in the war McLeod would increase his tally to 21 destroyed, 3 probables and 12 and 1 shared destroyed while flying as CO of No. 443 Sqn RCAF. He was eventually shot down and killed near Nijmegen on 27 September 1944 when he was bounced by nine Bf 109Gs. Although not the highest scoring Canadian ace of the war – that was George Beurling – McLeod was the leading RCAF ace as most of Beurling's victories were achieved while he was serving as an RAF pilot. (Wayne Ralph)

joint operations with monoplane German Bf 109s in Spain, and the success pilots had achieved in the conflict convinced senior officers in the *Regia Aeronautica* that manoeuvrability in a fighter was the key to success. Even future Air Force Chief of Staff General Francesco Pricolo reported in 1938 that 'all the pilots have expressed their conviction, which I share, that the usefulness of collective aerobatics has been most outstandingly confirmed in Spain'.

While many fighter units included a selection of combat veterans at the beginning of the war, they were handicapped by their belief that better manoeuvrability would be decisive in aerial combat. The vertical dive-and-zoom and cut-and-run tactics developed by the Luftwaffe in Spain were completely ignored. Unable to appreciate the changes that were taking place both technically and in the area of pilot training, the *Regia Aeronautica* would enter the war at a distinct disadvantage.

RAF PILOT TRAINING

For the RAF it was never an issue of numbers. Throughout the war it would always have enough volunteers to fill its ranks. Indeed, the glamorous and dashing image of the World War I ace had struck a chord with the British public that was fuelled by the press during the interwar period. When war broke out and the National Service Act came into force the prospect of compulsory military service pushed many young and talented men towards the more glamorous and somewhat 'safer' RAF. Unfortunately, the fictional image of the ace jarred with the reality of combat in the frontline, and this was particularly the case for those pilots sent to defend Malta. Living conditions on the island were also far from ideal either, especially when compared with those experienced by pilots flying from a Fighter Command airfield on the Channel front.

For the young volunteer, eager to jump into a Spitfire or Hurricane, the training process would come as a shock. Preparing young men to fly these powerful machines required a great deal of time and expert instruction. After volunteering for aircrew service many applicants were surprised to find themselves back at home and told to wait for their call-up letter. When they did receive it the new recruit would report to an Air Crew Reception Centre (ACRC), where they would spend between two and ten weeks. Given the classification 'aircrafthand second class' upon arriving at the ACRC, these aspiring fighter pilots would learn the basics of service life. After the successful completion of ACRC the new recruit would be sent to an Initial Training Wing (ITW). Here, building on the lessons learned at ACRC, recruits would hone their skills further with more detailed lessons on meteorology, principles of flight and drill.

In late 1941 an extra step was introduced to ITW in order to save time and resources. Short flying courses at an Elementary Flying School (EFS) were put on to give the new student a limited number of hours of dual instruction on de Havilland Tiger Moths or Miles Magisters. After about 12 hours of flying, students needed to show the necessary skills required to go 'solo'. If they could not they would be reassigned, thus saving the RAF valuable time and human resources at the later stages of training. Having shown aptitude for flight, and been promoted to the rank of leading aircraftsman, a successful trainee was now ready for more advanced flying training.

At the Elementary Flying Training School (EFTS) the young recruit would begin a prolonged flying programme using either the Tiger Moth or the Magister. Students would be taught the relatively simple, but vital, skills of straight and level flight, medium turns, climbing, diving and stall recovery. Once these skills had been mastered the student pilot would begin flying circuits. This involved taking off, climbing to a safe height and then flying straight and level downwind parallel to the runway. They would then turn and line up the aircraft with the runway, before carrying out a full stop landing. Having mastered these skills the student pilot would then fly his first solo. Further instruction would include spinning, formation flying and navigation. After successfully logging some 50 hours of flight time, half of which was solo, the new pilot would move on. Unfortunately, many students would fail EFTS and, sadly, a good number were listed as KIFA – Killed in Flying Accidents.

The next stage involved an increase in horsepower. Moving onto Service Flying Training (SFT), the student would be introduced to the North American Harvard or the Miles Master. Both were dual control and far more powerful with 550hp and 870hp engines respectively. These aircraft were more demanding too, and the first half of the course was repeat flights that had been carried out during EFTS. After a short period the student pilots were expected to solo. This was followed by further dual instruction, and night flying was added. If you could handle the Harvard or Master you were then judged able to fly a frontline fighter. To reach that point the student had to complete a further 120 hours (including 20 hours of night flying) during three-and-a-half months of flying. Finally, with 200 hours in his logbook, the cadet was awarded his wings.

Having survived to this point, the pilot's last step before being assigned to a fighter squadron was the Operational Training Unit (OTU). For those of the pre-war era and the first few months of World War II, frontline training occurred at squadron level. That meant new pilots would be posted to an operational unit with very little time on their assigned fighter and no tactical training of any sort. While this worked well before the war, combat attrition soon provoked a major change.

Because there were no two-seater Spitfires in which to give pilots their first flight, young trainees could only learn about the fighter by first familiarizing themselves with the controls and then taking it up for a solo flight. In some cases in 1939–40 trainee pilots missed out on larger monoplane instruction on Harvards and Masters and went straight onto the Spitfire or Hurricane instead. One such individual was future ace Tom Neil of No. 249 Sqn, who recalled:

We flew Spitfires straight from biplanes. None of us had flown monoplanes before and suddenly we were faced with these fearsome aeroplanes called Spitfires. And the bloke said to me, 'This is a Spitfire – get in and fly it'. All the training you had was to sit in the hanger with a blindfold covering your eyes and the Spitfire on trestles, and you felt round the cockpit trying to identify all the bits, pulling the wheels up and putting the flaps down. This lasted for just half a day, then you were introduced to your aeroplane and told to get on with it, and that was that.

By March 1940, however, two OTUs had been established and were equipped with a mixture of Hurricanes and Spitfires. Here, young aviators would learn to fly the aircraft they would use in combat, and by 1941 fighter pilots could expect to enter squadron service with a minimum of 270 hours of flight time.

By mid-1941 one of the war's most successful training operations was in full swing. Hundreds of aircrew were being trained overseas (in Canada, Australia, South Africa, New Zealand and Rhodesia) as part of the BCATP – a similar programme had also been established in the USA. The BCATP was truly remarkable, and it would be responsible for training nearly half the aircrew that served in the RAF, RCAF, RAAF, RNZAF and SAAF.

AIRCRAFT RECOGNITION

'People who regard Aircraft Recognition with a patronizing contempt, almost invariably die . . . GREATLY ASTONISHED'
The Aircrew Service Manual, August 1942

Unfortunately, it was very easy to mistake a friendly aircraft for an enemy machine during the stress, speed and confusion of combat. Pilots were told over and over again to 'never commit the fatal error of underestimating the importance of this subject. Though actual figures cannot, of course, be given, it may be stated that an amazing number of British aircraft have been lost through neither more nor less than faulty recognition'. Not only was recognition important in most if not all cases, seeing the enemy first often meant the difference between victory and death. Tragically the first fatalities suffered by RAF Fighter Command occurred when a Spitfire from No. 74 Sqn shot down two Hurricanes of No. 56 Sqn over Essex on 6 September 1939. Many pilots during the Malta campaign would mistake Bf 109s for C.202s, Re.2001s for Bf 109s and Spitfires for P-40s or Hurricanes.

Top Malta ace George Beurling was one of the few pilots who recognized the need for sound aircraft recognition at an early stage in his career as a fighter pilot, and during his training in England he worked on improving his eyesight:

I would pick out a hill in the distance, then a tree on that hill, then a branch of that tree and bring my eyes to focus on it and try to make out the details as quickly as possible. By doing that again and again, I found I could spot aircraft in the sky and distinguish what they were quicker than other fellows.

Beurling's ability to spot enemy aircraft before anyone else became legendary on Malta.

GUNNERY

At the outbreak of war RAF Fighter Command slowly found itself poorly served when it came to the combat

Success and survival in aerial combat often came down to the simple act of spotting the enemy first, and for those with exceptional eyesight this proved to be a major advantage. Pilots like George Beurling, who had phenomenal vision, could pick out enemy aircraft long before their squadronmates. With the enemy spotted, a pilot could then assess the situation and decide on the appropriate course of action. This dramatic Air Ministry vision training poster is succinct and unambiguous. For a young recruit this was probably the most important lesson to learn, and practice, before heading into combat. (Author)

HE WHO SEES FIRST LIVES LONGEST

Systematic **SCANNING** *is essential*

VISION TRAINING FOR AIRCREWS A.D.2824 SHEET 4

tactics it could employ against the enemy. The change from wooden, fabric-covered biplane fighters to all metal stress-skinned aircraft in the 1930s had altered the aerial landscape considerably. Like the biplane, the lessons learned from World War I were deemed to be obsolete and quickly discarded. However, as had been the case over the Western Front in 1918, agility and the fighter's ability to manoeuvre aggressively were soon revealed to again be the keys to success in aerial combat in World War II.

RAF tacticians also believed that Luftwaffe fighters like the Bf 109 lacked the range to be able to escort bombers successfully to targets in Britain (one of the reasons for the development of the Boulton Paul Defiant). Instead, Fighter Command pilots would be met by large numbers of German bombers in close formation that were protected by their interlocking fields of defensive fire. To counter the threat, the RAF kept their fighters in tight formations in order to mass their firepower. As a consequence early training did not focus on manoeuvring or gunnery. Finally, in June 1940, the RAF formalized air-to-air gunnery, giving young trainees their first chance to fire at a moving target. Unfortunately however, until late in the war, air-to-air gunnery training remained abysmal.

ITALIAN PILOT TRAINING

Italy entered the war with a false sense of accomplishment. The numerous pre-war world record flights had proven the nation's ability to produce sound aircraft and skilled pilots. As part of a well-orchestrated publicity campaign many believed the *Regia Aeronautica* to be a modern well-trained force. Unfortunately, when Italy entered

Until the late stages of the war Allied aerial gunnery training was not very good. Indeed, many of the pilots who arrived on Malta had received little or no training in the fine art of air-to-air gunnery prior to entering combat. For those that did have a chance to fire at a towed target, it was a brief affair with little or no time for improvement. And for pilots trained in Canada, that target was probably towed behind a garishly painted Fairey Battle. Here, marked up in the distinctive black and yellow target tug colour scheme, an obsolete Battle warms up on the snowy ramp at Mountain View gunnery school in Ontario, Canada. Battles flew tens of thousands of hours as part of the British Commonwealth Air Training Plan. (Author)

the war on 10 June 1940, the *Regia Aeronautica* was far from modern and was completely unprepared for a long conflict. Unsurprisingly, the same could be said for its pilot training system.

As with the curriculum followed by RAF Training Command, the instruction of future Italian fighter pilots was broken down into three stages – basic, advanced and operational. Not only did the Italians enter the war with an obsolete fighter force, its pilots received far less flying training hours than did their contemporaries in the RAF, Luftwaffe and the USAAF. Unlike the RAF, which rapidly expanded its training system to make good the attrition of 1940, the *Regia Aeronautica* had no similar sense of urgency. Its frontline units suffered accordingly as the war progressed.

In reality, expansion was out of the question due to the Italian aircraft industry's inability to provide the *Regia Aeronautica* with sufficient combat aeroplanes. Unable to acquire enough C.202s to supply its entire fighter force, it is hard to see how the *Regia Aeronautica* could have found the resources to expand its training programmes. Nevertheless, fighter pilots were being trained.

From 1938 to 1940 trainee pilots received 30 hours of initial flight training using the Breda Ba.25 biplane at the *Scuole di 1 Periodo* (basic flying training school). This changed in October 1940 when the number of hours was increased to 60, spread between several aircraft types – 30 hours in the AVIA FL.3, followed by 20 hours in the SAIMAN 202 and ten hours of aerobatics in either the CANSA C.5, SAIMAN 200 or Caproni Ca.164. After mastering these aircraft the trainee would be issued with a flight certificate and moved onto the IMAM Ro.41. With the completion of a further 25 hours on this light biplane fighter type the trainee pilot would receive a military certificate. It took roughly nine months to reach this point in the syllabus, successful candidates having emerged from an intake of around 1,600 cadets.

Instrument training was not introduced to the training programme until June 1941, and even then it consisted of a mere five hours of tuition.

With their military certificates in hand, the new trainees would be posted to one of three *Scuole di 2 Periodos* for their advanced pilot training. Here, students were

Powered by a single Alfa Romeo D2 240hp engine, the Breda Ba.25 biplane trainer served with the *Regia Aeronautica* from 1932 until the Italian armistice – despite production having ended after delivery of the 719th example to the air force in late 1938. All future fighter pilots would have to accrue 30 flying hours on the Ba.25 prior to being allowed to move on to more challenging aeroplane types. (Giorgio Apostolo)

introduced to the more powerful Fiat CR.30 or CR.32 biplane fighters. By mid-1942 pilots were accruing up to 85 hours of flying training at the advanced stage, but this was still inadequate when compared to what their Allies counterparts were receiving.

The third stage of training took place at an operational squadron, with new fighter pilots receiving up to 30 hours of aerobatic training. As the war progressed this part of the syllabus was not always made available. Wholly dependent on the leadership and skills of the individual squadron commander, the quality of aerobatic training given to a new pilot varied considerably. Combat tactics were not taught, but simulated combat situations were flown to ready the young pilot for operations. Such training would involve either pairs or sections of four aircraft, and these exercises were normally led by a combat-experienced or veteran pilot. Novice pilots could expect up to 50 hours of combat training.

The *Regia Aeronautica* deemed that 135 flying hours was sufficient to prepare a new pilot for combat. His equivalent in the RAF, by contrast, would have received between 150 and 200 hours prior to being posted to an operational squadron.

GUNNERY

Unfortunately for Italian fighter pilots gunnery training was considered unimportant, and many would learn how to use their weapons in combat! The only tuition given to aviators consisted of two exercises – the strafing of fixed ground targets and shooting at a cluster of free-floating balloons. There was no shooting at a moving target and deflection shooting was not even discussed. Ignoring the latter is particularly mystifying when when one considers that all armament in Italian fighters consisted of two machine guns mounted above the engine that were synchronized to fire between the propeller blades. This type of armament obviated the problems associated with wing-mounted guns and the variable accuracy of their converging fire, thus making deflection shooting considerably easier. This would have become obvious during the Spanish Civil War, but unfortunately for fighter pilots of the *Regia Aeronautica* these experiences were not incorporated into the training syllabus and exploited to good effect.

Obsolete fighters like the IMAM Ro.41 were put to good use by the *Regia Aeronautica's Scuole di 1 Periodo* flying school, which was established in 1938. A student pilot would begin his training on the Breda Ba.25 biplane, before moving onto the more powerful Ro.41. Originally conceived as a light fighter in 1934, the Ro.41 (of which 753 examples were built) was considered to be Italy's best intermediate trainer of the war. (Giorgio Apostolo)

Between 1940 and 1942 Anonima Vercellese Industria Aeronautica (AVIA) and Augusta built 335 FL.3s for the *Regia Aeronautica*. Powered by a 85hp Continental C-85 engine, the FL.3 was unique amongst Italian primary training aircraft due to its side-by-side seating. (Giorgio Apostolo)

The lack of instrument flight training that was previously mentioned would also hamper the fighter force's effectiveness during the early years of the war. Unable to operate in inclement weather, pilots of the *Regia Aeronautica* soon gained a reputation for being 'fair weather' fliers. They were also known for their unpredictability during combat, preferring to employ their aerobatic skills when engaging the enemy rather than the more simplified and effective dive-and-zoom tactics used by their German and British counterparts.

While the training methods may have been different the results were the same. Both the RAF and the *Regia Aeronautica* trained young men to be fighter pilots, which was an occupation fraught with danger and death. Not only did a young pilot have to master his machine – one that when not handled properly could kill him just as easily as combat – he also had to fight his war at high altitude in a completely alien environment. Pilots had to wear masks connected to a pressurized source of oxygen when flying at altitudes in excess of 10,000ft. Damage to this system could lead to oxygen deprivation or death. A pilot also had to be prepared to withstand extreme cold and discomfort at high altitude.

The cockpits of most fighters were also extremely cramped, with little room for movement. As a result, the effects of continuous muscle tension and sluggish blood circulation led to slower reactions and pain in the extremities. Pilots were also subject to the effects of extremely rapid changes in altitude when in a power dive, the increase in atmospheric pressure during such descents producing profound pain in the ears and sinuses. The pull up that followed was also a painful experience, with the powerful change in centrifugal force rapidly draining blood away from the brain. This caused disconcerting 'grey outs', total loss of vision or unconsciousness. Every pilot reacted differently to these forces, but in combat, when all of one's faculties were necessary, the loss of vision, even for a brief moment, often proved fatal.

For the British pilots, the constant attacks on Malta during 1941–42 meant flying two or three missions a day. The repeated scrambles, the frantic climb to altitude and diving attacks quickly took their toll both mentally and physically. In comparison, Italian pilots had a more leisurely routine in which one or two missions a day was the norm.

COMBAT

'With Malta in our hands, the British would have had little chance of exercising any further control over convoy traffic in the Central Mediterranean. It has the lives of many thousands of Germans and Italians on its conscience.'
Feldmarschall Erwin Rommel

As March 1942 drew to a close 31 Spitfire VBs had finally been added to the island's defences. Some 17 long months had past since the end of the Battle of Britain, but only now was the Spitfire being released for duty outside of the British Isles. Up to that point Malta's aerial defenders had made do with a mixed bag of Gladiators, Hurricanes and Fulmars. The island's commanders, while grateful for the Spitfire's long-awaited arrival, were still extremely anxious after intelligence reports referred to the arrival in Rome of General Kurt Student – Germany's top paratroop commander. Intelligence also indicated Hitler's intention of seizing Malta by the end of April in order to safeguard the sealanes for Rommel's new desert offensive.

The Luftwaffe's build up in Sicily had reached its peak by early April 1942, with close to 400 additional aircraft committed to the campaign. The Joint Intelligence Sub Committee of the Chiefs-of-Staff reported to the British Government that Malta's weakened state made it imminent for invasion. To add to the defenders' distress the first of 52 brand new C.202s from 9° and 10° *Gruppi*, 4° *Stormo* had been flown in to Sicily to commence offensive operations – as previously noted, the *Folgore* had first seen action over Malta between July and November 1941 in the hands of 9° *Gruppo*, 4° *Stormo*. The return of 4° *Stormo* greatly increased the size of the Axis fighter force (which up until then had consisted of approximately 95 Bf 109F-4s), putting even more pressure on Malta's dwindling defences.

The newly equipped 84ª *Squadriglia* shows off its Serie III C.202s at Undine airfield in February 1942. At the beginning of April the unit, as part of 10° *Gruppo*, 4° *Stormo*, was transferred to Castelvetrano airfield on Sicily to support bomber operations against Malta. This squadron was led by Capitano Franco Lucchini who 'made ace' by claiming two Spitfires destroyed over Malta on 5 and 15 May – he had previously scored three victories in North Africa in 1940–41. (Giorgio Apostolo)

On 19 April pilots from 10° *Gruppo* undertook their first acclimatization flight and suffered their first loss when Sergente Elio Trevisan of 90ª *Squadriglia* experienced a problem with his oxygen supply and was forced to bail out. He was subsequently picked up safely. This would prove to be a frequent problem for the C.202, resulting in unacceptably low serviceability rates.

By the third week of April punishing raids by both Luftwaffe and *Regia Aeronautica* units had reduced the number of serviceable Spitfires and Hurricanes on Malta to a mere handful. On the 19th seven more Hurricanes arrived from North Africa, these being the first RAF fighters seen in the air over the island in five days. The initial batch of Spitfires delivered during March had brought some relief, but there had been too few of them to conduct any sustained combat operations. Help was on the way, however.

On 1 April Prime Minister Winston Churchill had cabled US President Franklin D. Roosevelt directly and pressed his case for assistance in getting Spitfires to Malta. By using the US Navy carrier USS *Wasp* (CV-7) the RAF would be able to deliver 50 Spitfires to the island. Roosevelt agreed, and on 20 April Operation *Calendar* succeeded with the delivery of 46 of 47 Spitfires. The surprising and sudden arrival of so many aircraft breathed new life into the defences, although this would again be only a temporary fix.

The *Regia Aeronautica* and the Luftwaffe quickly responded later that same day by mounting 272 bomber sorties against Malta's three airfields – Takali, Luqa and Hal Far. The Italian contribution to the raid consisted of 19 C.202s from 10° *Gruppo's* 90ª *Squadriglia*. Unfortunately, just 30 minutes into the flight two C.202s collided, killing the formation leader and forcing his wingman to bail out into the sea. The mission was immediately aborted.

The persistent Luftwaffe attacks took a heavy toll. By 21 April only 27 Spitfires were still flyable, and this figure was reduced to 17 during the course of the day. Air Vice-Marshal Sir Hugh Lloyd, AOC Malta, was not impressed. After a quick inspection following the events of the 21st he found the condition of many of the remaining Spitfires left much to be desired. Guns were dirty and had not been fired since they were installed in the UK and many radios were not working. Lloyd's harshest critique, however, fell on the new pilots. In his message to HQ Fighter Command he said bluntly, 'Only fully experienced operational pilots must come here. It is no place for beginners. Casualties up to now have been the beginners.'

Pilots with limited experience were not just exclusive to the British. The Italians had their fare share of novice aviators as well, although some did better than others. One such pilot was Sergente Bruno Lentini of 53° *Stormo*, who not only survived his first mission but also claimed his first Spitfire destroyed during the course of the sortie:

On my first mission over Malta I was still pretty inexperienced. I was flying a C.202 with 374ª *Squadriglia* 'Asso di Bastoni' ('Ace of Clubs'). I was placed at the far right of the formation. At a height of 8,000m we came across the German bombers, which we were meant to protect. They flew some 1,000m below us. Our task was to shield them while they were flying over and bombing Malta.

After the German bombers had dropped their bombs, they turned back, and so did my squadronmates. I was sort of spellbound watching the island of Malta beneath me when I noticed I was flying off course. All of a sudden my captain yelled at me in my headset – 'You stupid boy, you have two Spitfires on your tail!' I saw the tracks of their machine gun fire and decided to nose-dive. This sudden move disoriented the two pilots who were chasing me. I nose-dived some 4,000m and then disappeared into the clouds. When I flew back into clear sky I found that I was on the tail of the two Spitfires, so I instinctively fired at them and hit one. I saw the aeroplane catch fire and plummet into the sea. I prayed for the pilot to jump but he never did. I felt so guilty about killing someone, although he had of course tried to kill me just minutes earlier.

Back at base I was admonished for leaving the formation, but I was not grounded, for fighter pilots were in constant demand to fly escort missions and convoy protection literally round the clock.

The heavy attacks on the three RAF airfields would continue unabated throughout the rest of April, with devastating results. On the 27th the C.202s of 4° *Stormo* made their biggest showing to date when 27 *Folgores* escorted 35 Ju 88s, 21 Ju 87s and five Z1007bis

Amongst the first Spitfires to be flown into Malta was Mk VB AB264, the aircraft being one of 15 fighters flown off *Eagle* during Operation *Spotter* on 7 March 1942. Issued to No. 249 Sqn, AB264 would be credited with the destruction of a Ju 87 on 25 March and the shared destruction of a Ju 88 the following day. The fighter later served with Nos. 185, 1435 and 229 Sqns whilst on Malta, before being passed on to the Twelfth Air Force in October 1943. (Frederick Galea)

SPITFIRE VC COCKPIT

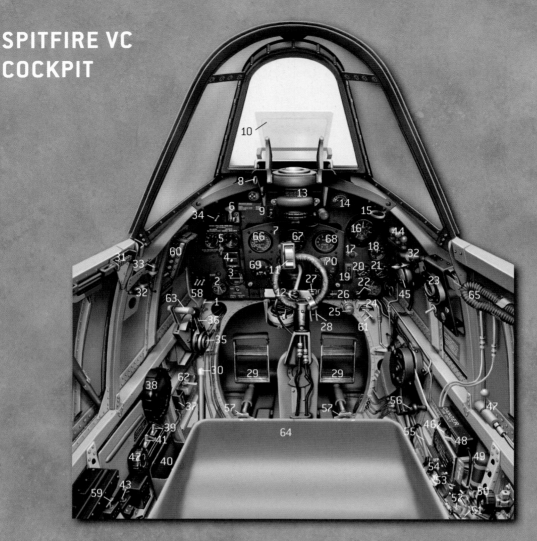

1. Boost control cut-out
2. Brake triple pressure gauge
3. Elevator tabs position indicator
4. Undercarriage position indicator
5. Oxygen regulator
6. Flaps control
7. Blind flying instrument panel
8. Lifting ring for sunscreen
9. Reflector gunsight switch
10. Sunscreen
11. Gun and cannon three-position push button
12. Camera-gun push button
13. Barr and Stroud GM 2 reflector gunsight
14. Voltmeter
15. Ventilator control
16. Tachometer
17. Fuel pressure warning lamp
18. Boost pressure gauge
19. Oil pressure gauge
20. Oil temperature gauge

21. Radiator temperature gauge
22. Fuel contents gauge and push button
23. Remote contactor and switch
24. Slow-running cut-out
25. Engine priming pump
26. Engine starting pushbutton
27. Booster coil pushbutton
28. Fuel cock control
29. Rudder pedals
30. Radiator flap control lever
31. Two-position door catch
32. Cockpit floodlight
33. Camera indicator supply plug
34. Navigation lights switch
35. Control friction adjusters
36. Propeller speed control lever
37. Radio control plug storage
38. Elevator trimming tab handwheel
39. Camera-gun switch
40. Map case

41. Pressure head heater switch
42. Rudder trimming tab handwheel
43. Oil dilution push button
44. Stowage for reflector gunsight lamps
45. Signalling switchbox
46. R.3002 Identification Friend or Foe (IFF) master pushbuttons
47. Harness release control
48. R.3002 IFF master switch
49. CO2 cylinder for emergency lowering of undercarriage
50. Oxygen supply cock
51. Windscreen de-icing pump
52. Windscreen de-icing needle valve
53. Undercarriage emergency lowering control
54. Windscreen de-icing cock
55. External fuel tank jettison lever

56. Undercarriage control unit lever
57. Rudder pedal stand adjusting wheels
58. Ignition switches
59. Signal discharger control
60. T.R. 1196 or T.R. 1304 transmitter and receiver controls
61. Fuel tank pressurizing cock control
62. Air intake control (Seafire and Spitfire VC Trop only)
63. Throttle control
64. Seat
65. Oxygen hose
66. Airspeed indicator
67. Artificial horizon
68. Rate-of-climb indicator
69. Altimeter
70. Turn-and-slip indicator

C.202 *FOLGORE*
COCKPIT

1. San Giorgio Type B reflector gunsight
2. Clock
3. Boost gauge
4. Compass
5. Fuel cock
6. Gun cocking handle (left)
7. Airspeed indicator
8. Turn-and-slip indicator
9. Artificial horizon
10. Gun cocking handle (right)
11. Vertical speed indicator
12. Coolant temperature
13. Oil temperature
14. Gun charge indicators
15. Altimeter
16. Rev counter

17. Oil pressure gauge
18. Fuel pressure gauge
19. Magneto switch
20. Engine cut out
21. Magneto retard
22. Main starter switch
23. Undercarriage position indicator
24. Undercarriage indicator switch
25. Safety release handle
26. Oxygen flow indicator
27. Oxygen pressure gauge
28. Flap position indicator
29. Undercarriage selector lever
30. Brake pressure gauge
31. Wing guns ammunition rounds counter

32. Hydraulic circuit pressure gauge
33. Tank air pressure gauge
34. Fuselage guns ammunition rounds counter
35. Dynamo main switch
36. Oxygen economizer
37. Fuel contents gauge
38. Engine priming pump
39. Engine starting switch
40. Cockpit lamp
41. Undercarriage warning horn
42. Electrical switch and fuse box
43. Tailwheel lock handle
44. Flap selector
45. Emergency hydraulic pump
46. Propeller speed control

47. Throttle control
48. Flap control lever
49. Oil cooler flap control lever
50. Pneumatic pressure reducer
51. Trim wheel
52. Coolant radiator flap indicator
53. Rudder bar and pedals
54. Control column
55. Seat
56. Allocchio Bacchini B.30 receiver/transmitter switch box
57. Pitot tube heater switch

in raids on Luqa, Takali and the Grand Harbour. With no RAF fighters available to intercept the incoming Italian formation, the defence of Malta rested exclusively with the island's overworked anti-aircraft batteries. By the end of April just seven Spitfires and a handful of Hurricanes remained serviceable. All three airfields had been savagely pounded, with Takali receiving 841 tons of bombs alone. The defending fighters were credited with 53 victories during the month, but none of these were C.202s.

The Allied reinforcement of Malta from the air would continue, nevertheless. Flying off the carriers *Wasp* (50 Spitfires) and HMS *Eagle* (17 Spitfires) on 9 May, 61 fighters would make it safely to the island. This time the Malta-based personnel were better prepared for their new arrivals. Once on the ground, individual aircraft would make for their assigned aircraft pen. There, five groundcrew would immediately strip the Spitfire of its long range tank and refuel it. A replacement pilot would then strap into the fighter and immediately take to the air. This new system worked well, for despite there being nine Axis raids on fighter bases on Malta that day no Spitfires were destroyed on the ground.

On the second to last raid of the day the first C.202 to be claimed shot down by a Spitfire pilot was credited to future Australian ace Plt Off John Bisley of No. 126 Sqn. He had been in one of 33 Spitfires that had been scrambled to intercept a formation of five Z1007bis bombers, with an escort of 16 C.202s, detected approaching the island at 1745hrs. The defenders enthusiastically claimed three Cants and one C.202 destroyed, with a second *Folgore* damaged. The overoptimistic claims, however, did not stand up to scrutiny, for only one Cant was badly damaged and a C.202 was hit by a single 20mm shell. The Italians

also overclaimed, being credited with three Spitfires shot down and one damaged. All of the RAF fighters landed without having suffered any damage.

9 May was undoubtedly one of the most successful days in the defence of Malta. A total of 61 Spitfires had arrived safely, and during the frenetic fighting that had followed their arrival only four had been shot down, with six more damaged on the ground. By nightfall, counting the Spitfires already on the island, the defenders had at least 50 Supermarine fighters, and a handful of Hurricanes, ready for operations on 10 May. Although the Axis units had in turn suffered modest losses, not a single C.202 had been downed.

10 May 1942 would prove to be a critical date in the defence of Malta. No fewer than five Spitfire squadrons (Nos. 126, 185, 249, 601 and 603) were ready for battle that morning, and as the first raid approached the island the defences reacted like never before. No longer resigned to sending just a handful of fighters into the fray, the RAF scrambled 37 Spitfires and 13 Hurricanes. 10 May would also see the first confirmed destruction of a C.202 by a Spitfire.

After several Luftwaffe raids by Ju 87s and Ju 88s, the *Regia Aeronautica* put in an appearance at 1810hrs when five Z1007bis, with an escort of 20 C.202s from 4° *Stormo* and ten Re.2001s from 2° *Gruppo*, approached the island. The Italian aircraft were followed in by German Ju 87s, with a large escort of Bf 109s. To meet the threat 42 Spitfires were scrambled, with aircraft from No. 601 Sqn being the first to attack. Within minutes a Z1007bis had been shot down, as was the C.202 of Capitano Roberto Dagasso, CO of 97ᵃ *Squadriglia*. He had fallen victim to New Zealander Plt Off Wally Caldwell (flying BR344/4-H) of No. 601 Sqn.

By dusk on 10 May, the Spitfire pilots had claimed three Ju 88s, nine Ju 87s, two Bf 109s, one Z1007bis and one C.202 destroyed – these successes were very similar to

9 May 1942 would see the year's largest delivery of Spitfires to Malta when, as part of Operation *Bowery*, *Eagle* and *Wasp* launched 64 Spitfires between them – 61 fighters arrived safely on Malta. Twenty of the Spitfire Mk VC Trops embarked in the US Navy carrier can be seen here below deck in *Wasp's* cavernous hangar bay. BR136, closest to the camera, would serve with Nos. 249 and 601 Sqns. It then moved to No. 59 Repair and Salvage Unit and was finally written off when it crashed on take off from Sorman West airfield, in Libya, on 2 April 1943. (Author)

GEORGE BEURLING

Nicknamed 'Screwball', George Beurling was the highest-scoring ace during the siege of Malta. He was also one of the greatest Allied aces of World War II. Born to a Swedish father and English mother in Montreal, Canada, on 6 December 1921, George was a complicated man who left a lasting impression on all those that met him, even briefly. In 1930 Beurling took his first flight. Eight years later, at the age of 16, he went solo whilst at the controls of a Curtiss-Reid Rambler biplane. Leaving high school shortly thereafter, Beurling got a job as a co-pilot with an airfreight company in Gravenhurst, Ontario. He soon grew bored of this, however, and after seeing a newspaper article describing the handful of American volunteers heading to China to fight the Japanese, he gave in his notice. Unfortunately for Beurling he was arrested for attempting to enter the US illegally.

(Photo courtesy of author)

With Europe now at war Beurling went straight to his local RCAF recruiter. The latter was unprepared for such a large influx of volunteers, and many, including Beurling, were turned away. Unperturbed, he then tried enlisting in the Finnish Air Force so as to help the small Scandinavian country defend itself from Soviet invasion. Beurling was accepted, but his father refused to sign the necessary papers. In May 1940 Beurling worked his way across the Atlantic to join the RAF. Failing to take his birth certificate with him, the young Canadian was turned away yet again. Returning home to find the necessary paperwork, Beurling was soon on his way back to Scotland. Finally, in September 1940, the RAF accepted him into its ranks.

Following a year of training Beurling was initially posted to the RCAF's No. 403 Sqn, However, a decision that RCAF units should be manned exclusively by RCAF personnel saw Beurling, who was part of the RAF, posted to No. 41 Sqn — both units were equipped with Spitfire VBs. His first victory occurred on 1 May 1942 when he shot down an Fw 190. Expecting to be praised and congratulated for his first kill, Beurling was instead reprimanded for deliberately breaking formation. Considered a lone wolf and unpopular with his superiors, Beurling was soon transferred to No. 249 Sqn on Malta — then dubbed 'the fighter pilot's paradise' — in June 1942.

Those who flew with him were stunned by his phenomenal eyesight, and many felt safe knowing that they would never be bounced by the enemy. Beurling was neither a smoker or a drinker, and he was never heard to swear either — his prime expletive was 'screwball', hence his nickname.

The month after he arrived on Malta, the young Canadian claimed 15 enemy aircraft destroyed (six of them C.202s) and six damaged. After his eighth victory he was awarded the Distinguished Flying Medal, followed by a Bar to this at the end of July. At the end of September, with his score standing at 21.333 victories, Beurling (who had reluctantly accepted a commission to pilot officer the previous month) received the Distinguished Flying Cross. The October 'Blitz' provided Beurling with another target-rich environment. In just five days he shot down eight aircraft (none of these were C.202s, however), the last three on the 14th. That same day he was shot down while attempting to intercept a large enemy formation in Spitfire VB BR173/T-D. Hit in the right heel by a cannon splinter, he parachuted into the sea and was soon rescued. Awarded the Distinguished Service Order shortly thereafter, Beaurling was sent back to the UK on 31 October and then posted home to Canada (whilst on temporary loan to the RCAF) on leave in November.

Returning to England in 1943, Beurling became an instructor at No. 61 OTU in July. Transferring to the RCAF, he was posted to No. 403 Sqn and claimed another victory on 24 September flying a Spitfire IX. Later posted to No. 412 Sqn, Beurling would score his final victory on 30 December 1943 for a total of 31.333 kills. one shared and nine damaged.

A maverick who was unable to come to terms with authority, Beurling was allowed to retire from the RCAF on 16 October 1944. Restless in civilian life, he signed up to fly as a volunteer with the new Israeli Air Force. Tasked with ferrying a Noorduyn Norseman across Europe to Israel, as Beurling departed Rome in the aircraft on 20 May 1948 it blew up, killing both him and his co-pilot. Sabotage was suspected but never proven.

FURIO DOGLIO NICLOT

Furio Doglio Niclot was Italy's most successful fighter pilot of the 1942 Malta campaign. Born in Calgliari on 24 April 1908, Niclot studied aeronautical engineering and, by 1930, had obtained his civil pilot's licence. Well qualified and a gifted aviator, he was soon employed as a test pilot and instructor by the Compania Nazionale Aeronautica. Flying from Rome's Littorio airport, he set his first world record on 28 December 1932 when he flew a Fiat AS.1 floatplane to an altitude of 24,154ft. More records would follow, and during 1933 he would complete his national service with the *Regia Aeronautica* as a non-commissioned Sottotente Pilota.

Upon his return to civilian life in 1935, Niclot became Breda's chief test pilot. He achieved further accolades flying aircraft from his new employer, using a Ba.33 to take the top prize in the Littorio Rally and, in 1937, breaking the world speed record in the Ba.88 ground attack prototype.

With war declared Niclot (having been given the rank of Capitano) returned to active service flying G.50s with 353ª *Squadriglia*, 20° *Gruppo*, 51° *Stormo*. His first combat assignment would be with the less than successful *Corpo Aereo Italiano* (CAI) expedition of late 1940. Flying from bases in Belgium, the CAI was Mussolini's ill-fated contribution to the Battle of Britain. Niclot never got to fire his guns in anger on the Channel front and returned to Italy in early 1941. Transferred to North Africa in April, Niclot scored his first victory on 30 June while flying escort for a flight of German Ju 87s. Engaging three Hurricanes, he shot one down and damaged another. He was awarded the Italian Bronze Medal for Military Valour following this action. Promoted to command of 151ª *Squadrigla* on 20 November 1941, Niclot led the unit home one month later to oversee its conversion to the C.202.

By June 1942 both Mussolini and the Luftwaffe were eager to neutralize Malta once and for all. On the 24th of that month the *Regia Aeronautica* began to reinforce its units on Sicily by posting in the HQ flight of 20° *Gruppo*, 51° *Stormo* and its three *Squadriglie* – including Capitano Niclot's 151ª *Squadrigla*. On 2 July Niclot scored his first Spitfire victory. Flying close escort for S.84bis

bombers, ten C.202s from Niclot's unit were intercepted by 11 Spitfires from Nos. 249 and 185 Sqn. During a head-on attack Sgt C. S. G. de Nancrede, flying Spitfire VC BR377/T-K of No. 249 Sqn, was hit by fire from Niclot's C.202 and subsequently crash-landed at Takali.

Niclot's combat experience over Malta was to be short but productive. Between 2 and 13 July he claimed six Spitfires shot down and two more shared destroyed with his wingman Maresciallo Ennio Tarantola. These daily dogfights took a heavy toll, however, and on 27 July Niclot fought his last battle. Leading 13 C.202s from 11°, 20° and 155° *Gruppi* that were charged with escorting nine German Ju 88s heading for the airfield at Takali, Niclot's fighters were intercepted by six Spitfires from No. 249 Sqn. The fourth C.202 in the lead formation of four aircraft was hit hard by a deadly accurate deflection shot fired by Sgt George Beurling (in BR301/UF-S), giving the Canadian his 13th victory. Seconds later he turned his attention to the lead fighter, flown by Niclot. The Italian ace did not see him coming, and according to Beurling 'The poor devil simply blew to pieces in the air' after he had fired a single burst at his target. Niclot was in fact trapped in the cockpit of C.202 '151-1', and he was killed seconds later when it crashed into the sea.

As one of Italy's leading fighter pilots he was posthumously awarded the *Medaglia d'Oro* (Gold Medal for Military Valour).

(Photo courtesy of Giorgio Apostolo)

Blast pens were vital for the survival of fighter aircraft on the ground. Only a direct hit or near miss at the entrance could destroy or damage an aircraft while in a pen. Those on Malta were made with various materials – the ones seen here at Takali, protecting two Spitfire VCs from No. 229 Sqn, were made out of sand bags. Others were constructed from empty fuel cans or limestone blocks recovered from bombed-out buildings. The extreme wear and tear of combat can clearly be seen on Spitfire EP691 in the foreground, which had been flown into Malta on 17 August 1942 as part of Operation *Baritone*. Ace Plt Off Colin Parkinson claimed a Bf 109 destroyed, a Ju 88 as a shared probable and a 'Breda 205' damaged whilst at the controls of EP691 on 12 October 1942. The Spitfire was itself lost on operations on 23 January 1943. (Frederick Galea)

the losses admitted by the Axis units. In return, the Italian fighter pilots claimed six RAF fighters shot down. However, only three Spitfires had been lost that day (none to C.202s), with six more being slightly damaged. The Italians exacted some revenge for this loss on 14 May when three Spitfires were credited to pilots from 2° and 9° *Gruppi*, and Australian ace Sgt 'Tony' Boyd of No. 185 Sqn was indeed shot down and killed. He may have fallen victim to a Bf 109F from III./JG 53, however.

15 May would see the greatest number of C.202s shot down to date. Some 30 *Folgores* from 4° *Stormo* were escorting three S.84bis bombers targeting the Fort Campbell barracks in St Paul's Bay at 0915hrs when they were intercepted by 12 Spitfires from Nos. 249 and 603 Sqns. In the resulting dogfight the Italians claimed four Spitfires shot down, but there were no losses on the British side. No. 249 Sqn's Flt Sgt Plt Off Lawrie Verrall fired an accurate burst into the Macchi flown by Capitano Alberto Argenton, commander of 91ª *Squadriglia*, who was killed when the fighter hit the sea.

A few hours later a single reconnaissance Ju 88, and its Bf 109 and C.202 escorts, was engaged off the island. Future Australian ace Sgt Jack Yarra of No. 603 Sqn took on the escort screen, noting in his Combat Report, 'Engaged seven 109s, damaged leader, was attacked by four 202s. Shot down one, who collided with his No. 2. Fought the remaining two until out of ammo'. Three days later Yarra would 'make ace' when he claimed two Bf 109s shot down. The newly arrived Spitfires were making their presence felt.

Despite the significant losses of 10 May, Feldmarschall Albert Kesselring, Commander-in-Chief, South, convinced himself that Malta was no longer a threat. Having informed Hitler that the Luftwaffe and the *Regia Aeronautica* had suffered only modest losses in the recent blitz on the island, Kesselring was told to reduce air operations over Malta and begin the transfer of aerial assets to North Africa and the Eastern Front. In mid-May three *Jagdgeschwader* would be transferred out, along with a number of bomber units. The *Regia Aeronautica* was also anxious to increase its strength in North Africa, duly ordering 4° *Stormo* to Libya. To compensate for this move, 155° *Gruppo*, 51° *Stormo* was transferred to Sicily from Rome. On 18 May Maggiore Duilio Fanali led the *Gruppo's* three *squadriglie* (351ª, 360ª and 378ª *Squadriglie*) to Gela.

Seventeen more Spitfires also arrived on Malta on the 18th as part of Operation *LB*, these machines flying off *Eagle*.

RAF TACTICS

American Plt Off Reade Tilley became an ace over Malta with seven victories, three probably destroyed and six damaged (two of which were C.202s) to his name.

In August 1942 he was transferred to the USAAF, and subsequently returned home. Here, Tilley wrote a lengthy paper describing the tactics used over Malta. A small excerpt from his report read as follows:

> By this stage of the war the RAF used the section 'four line abreast' battle formation, similar to the *Schwarm* employed by the Luftwaffe, with aircraft flying about 800 yards apart. A squadron comprised three such sections, typically with Red Section in the lead and with White and Blue Sections to the left and right of it, slightly above and 500-700 yards behind.
>
> Squadron commanders must bear in mind that the squadron has to be intact to do maximum damage to the enemy in combat – to this end, throttle back and even turn towards straggling sections while climbing to meet the enemy. There is no better feeling than to arrive at 25,000ft with the full squadron properly deployed, and then start hunting.
>
> In sections 'four line abreast' each aircraft watches the others' tails, above and below, and in doing so all four cover each other. One further advantage of this formation is that if one man is attacked, the man next to him is at the exact distance where he can throttle back and fire at the attacker from the beam.

On 25 July Air Vice-Marshal Keith Park, who had replaced Air Vice-Marshal Hugh Lloyd as AOC Malta just 11 days earlier, issued his 'Fighter Interception Plan' to his pilots. Up to this point the defending fighters had flown south of the island in order to gain height prior to attacking the enemy bomber formations approaching from the north. This usually meant that Axis aircraft were not engaged until after they had made their bomb runs. The devastation being caused by the bombers (34 aircraft had been damaged while on the ground in the first two weeks of July alone) had to be stopped, so Park issued the order that his pilots were to intercept incoming raids north of the island, well out to sea. Park's post-war biographer, Vincent Orange, summarised the order as follows:

> The sector controller was to ensure that his first squadron got its height up-sun and then intercepted the enemy's high fighter cover. The second squadron was to intercept the bombers' close escort or the bombers themselves, if unescorted. The third squadron was to make a head-on attack on the bombers about ten miles north of the coast, followed by a quarter attack, to force them to drop their bombs into the sea.

American Plt Off Reade Tilley arrived on Malta with No. 601 Sqn as part of Operation *Calendar* on 20 April 1942. His previous spell in the front line with No. 121 'Eagle' Sqn on the Channel front prepared him well for combat in the central Mediterranean, as he quickly claimed a series of kills once he had joined No. 126 Sqn's American flight in early May. Achieving ace status on 23 May with a Re.2001 destroyed (this was possibly a C.202 – he also claimed at least two *Folgores* damaged whilst on Malta), Tilley was awarded a DFC at this time as a result of his numerous aerial successes – seven destroyed, two probables and five damaged over Malta. (via Reade Tilley)

The changing of the Guard. On 15 July 1942 Air Vice-Marshal Keith Park (right) arrived on Malta to take over command of the island's air defence from Air Vice-Marshal Hugh Lloyd (left), who was now tour-expired. Lloyd was a former bomber pilot who had been brought in to build up Malta's offensive capacity, and had seen the island through the worst days of the siege. However, it was felt by some of the more senior fighter pilots on the island that he never really understood how best to use the Hurricane and Spitfire squadrons at his disposal, or was sympathetic to their operational requirements. Air Vice-Marshal Park, who had commanded No. 11 Group during the Battle of Britain, was very much a fighter pilot's advocate. He soon implemented the Fighter Interception Plan, which called for the forward interception of raids to the north of the island before the bombers hit their targets. (Imperial War Museum (CM 3068))

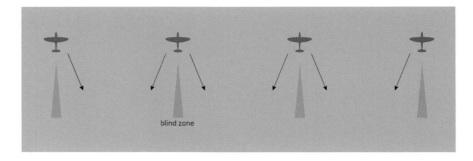

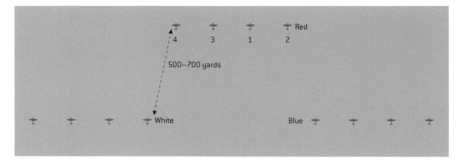

TOP
By 1942 the RAF routinely used the section 'four line abreast' battle formation, each aircraft flying with 80 yards' separation. This was similar to the highly successful Schwarm formation that had been employed by the Luftwaffe since the start of the war. The shaded areas immediately behind each Spitfire indicate the pilot's blind spot. In 'four line abreast' each pilot watched the others tail, both above and below. The arrows indicate which direction each pilot was responsible for covering.

BOTTOM
The standard squadron-strength 12 aircraft formation was made up of 'Red' Section flying lead, with 'White' and 'Blue' Sections to the left and right, slightly above and 500–700 yards behind.

The Italians closely monitored the air-to-ground communications to decipher where the Spitfires were heading. To throw them off, a decoder wheel was created in order to keep communication between pilots and fighter controllers as short as possible. This wheel was used by Flt Sgt Ian Maclennan. How it actually worked is unknown. (Wayne Ralph)

By month end, Air Vice-Marshal Park's new tactics had born fruit, with at least 22 Ju 88s and six Italian bombers having been shot down.

Shooting down one's opponent was the last stage in a well-orchestrated interception. The Spitfire was probably the best pure interceptor of the war, but its success was dependent on radar and an efficient fighter control system. Without it the Spitfires would not have been nearly as successful. Canadian Malta ace Plt Off Ian Maclennan of No. 1435 Sqn strongly believed that it was the contributions of the many rather than the few that produced the victory over Malta. He felt that most of the credit belonged to the experienced fighter controllers in the operations room near Salina Bay, codenamed 'Gondor', and the laminated decoding wheel carried by every pilot. 'Without the ground controllers and the code wheel, as well as the line abreast formation, we could never have won the battle of Malta'.

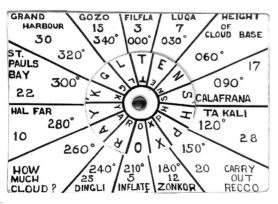

ITALIAN TACTICS

By 1942 the *Regia Aeronautica* had gained valuable combat experience, albeit at a heavy price. Unfortunately, what was learned was not fully implemented. The Italian predilection for individual fighter tactics based on aerobatic techniques remained. Any changes that did occur were usually driven by individual squadron commanders in the field and not from any systematic change in the training syllabus.

Fighter units typically went into action flying in outdated 'V' formations of between three and 12 aircraft. Approaching

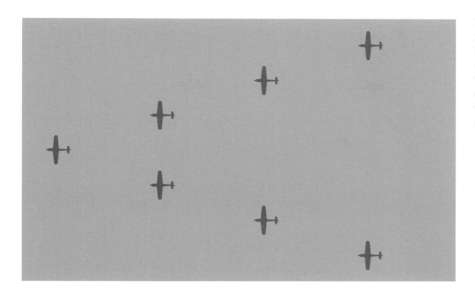

Throughout the aerial battles over Malta from June 1940 through to late October 1942, Italian fighter units continued to use the dated 'V' formation. In preparation for combat, however, pilots usually fanned their aircraft out into a line abreast formation.

the target, the aircraft would move into a 'right wing' abreast formation. Later in the war the leader–wingman formation was adopted.

During a 1943 interview, George Beurling gave a somewhat contradictory view regarding his Italian opponents, and the tactics they employed:

> The 'Eyeties' are comparatively easy to shoot down. Oh, they're brave enough. In fact, I think the 'Eyeties' have more courage than the Germans, but their tactics aren't so good. They are very good gliders, but they try to do clever aerobatics and looping. But they will stick with it even if things are going against them, whereas the 'Jerries' will run. Italian pilots were also handicapped by the 'anaemic' armament of their fighters.

What the leading Italian aces who fought over Malta were able to accomplish is a testament to their courage, skill and marksmanship. Armed with just two 12.7mm machine guns synchronized to fire between the propeller blades, the C.202 was handicapped by both a slow rate-of-fire and weight-of-fire. Any sort of aerial victory would have been either a lucky shot or accomplished at extremely close range. Fortunately for the RAF this meant that more Spitfires were damaged than shot down when C.202 pilots did indeed manage to get into a firing position.

The Italians did, however, have a major advantage over their British counterparts – health. While the C.202 pilots flew one or two missions a day, those defending Malta often flew three times. And not only were their lives threatened in the air, they could just as easily be killed on the ground. There was no sense of being safe at any time. And even when Malta's defences improved during the course of 1942, life on the island still remained extremely tough both in and out of the cockpit. Relief convoys struggled to get through the Axis blockade of the Mediterranean, forcing rations to be cut. For pilots, a daily ration consisted of nine ounces of locally made bread and corned beef that those who had to eat it said had been tinned during World War I!

If you were not killed by the enemy, illness and malnutrition would slowly take their toll. The constant scrambles, coupled with the incessant bombing and lack of

Unlike their Allied counterparts, fighter pilots of the *Regia Aeronautica* rarely marked their aircraft with individual victory markings. This photograph proves that there were exceptions to this rule, however, as Tenente Giovanni Ambrosio of 378ª *Squadriglia* poses with the single Spitfire silhouette he helped apply to the tail of his Serie III C.202 MM7841. This victory was credited to the pilot following an action on 10 July 1942 when Ambrosio, Sergente Maggiore Giovanni Fabbro and Sergente Maggiore Francesco Visentini claimed two Spitfires shot down. RAF losses for the day reveal that only a single fighter (from No. 126 Sqn) was destroyed. (Giorgio Apostolo)

food, meant that all fighter pilots became progressively thinner and weaker. Almost all who served on the island succumbed to illness and battle fatigue. Losing 20–30lb was commonplace. Bouts of severe dysentery, nicknamed the 'Malta Dog', plagued Malta in 1942, as did sand-fly fever and jaundice. Outwardly, pilots also looked more and more haggard as the year progressed. Often dressed for comfort rather then regulation, they were a tired lot with unshaven faces, long hair, bad skin and an assortment of open sores and bites all over their bodies.

The psychological effects of combat also took a heavy toll. Watching friends and comrades die, both in the air and on the ground, would tear into a man's soul and cast dark shadows of doubt in one's mind. While the RAF officially recognized the mental stresses and strains associated with combat, it was left to individual pilots to develop their own strategies for coping with these afflictions. Rest and relaxation was almost non-existent. Alcohol was available, but it was difficult to obtain and of questionable quality, and female companionship was highly unlikely.

In stark contrast, the C.202 pilots of the *Regia Aeronautica* lived in a world of luxury on Sicily. Even though they shared the same threat of sudden death in combat, their bases were a safe haven in which to relax and unwind. Italian fighter airfields were well stocked with good food and Italian wine. After a combat mission an Italian pilot could look forward to a hot meal and a shower, a good night's rest and, in some cases, female companionship. While fatigue was a constant threat, the Italians had more time out of the cockpit and better living conditions in which to recover. Their morale was also very good, as Ronaldo Scaroni of 151ª *Squadriglia* recalled:

It was clear not only from the number of new aeroplanes flying in, but from the calibre of the aircrews, that the High Command was serious about winning, and that was a big boost to everyone's morale. We knew we had the English badly outnumbered and we didn't see how we could possibly lose. There was a feeling that the whole thing would be over by the end of the summer at the latest. Our morale could not have been better. We were certain we were going to crush Malta and win the war. I can remember listening to Rome radio every night, hearing about yet another Axis victory. Whether it was us, the Germans or the Japanese, we were winning everywhere. It was uncanny.

By June 1942 it was clear that if the island were to succumb, it would not be due to an aerial assault. The only avenues left to the Axis were invasion or total blockade, both of which were beyond the resources available. June would also see a changing of the guard. The Spitfire pilots who had flown in during March were now tour expired and sent back for the UK. Their replacements would include a number of future aces, including George Beurling, who would join No. 249 Sqn.

For much of the month Axis bombing activity took the form of low-level attacks by *Jabos* (Bf 109s equipped with bombs) and fighter sweeps by C.202s.

By mid-June 213 Spitfire Vs had been delivered to Malta. Up to that point combat had seen 55 of them shot down, a further 16 crash-landed due to combat damage and 35 destroyed on the ground by enemy bombing. That left 92 serviceable machines split between five units, with the remaining aircraft being overhauled. By the end of the month the defenders had been credited with 52 victories and 13 probables.

July would open with a new Italian offensive. In support of their allies the Germans would transfer several highly experienced fighter and bomber units from the Eastern Front and North Africa to Sicily, including more Bf 109s from I./JG 77. The number of C.202s would, however, remain the same. The new July attacks again targeted Malta's airfields, and the increase in the tempo of attacks allowed Sgt George Beurling to open his scoring in spectacular fashion.

On the 6th Beurling would make his presence felt by shooting down three fighters and damaging a bomber. To meet the second raid of the day (three Z1007bis escorted by 24 C.202s of 20° *Gruppo* and 14 Re.2001s of 2° *Gruppo*), 11 Spitfires from No. 249 Sqn were scrambled. Yet more C.202s, led by Capitano Furio Doglio Niclot of 151ª *Squadriglia*, were also over the island flying a sweep ahead of the bombers. Beurling (in Spitfire BR323/S) met the incoming bombers head on, scoring strikes as he swept past. The C.202s of 20° *Gruppo* then engaged the Spitfires, with Beurling finding his mark early:

As the bombers turned to run I saw a Macchi 202 boring up on 'Smitty's' [Flg Off John Smith] tail. I did a quick climbing turn and bored in on the 'Eyetie', catching him unawares. A one-second burst smacked him in the engine and glycol tank. He burst into flames and went down like a plummet.

A pair of C.202s from 360ª *Squadriglia*, 155° *Gruppo*, 51° *Stormo* in formation over the Mediterranean in August 1942. Based at Gela, on Sicily, 155° *Gruppo* would see plenty of action over Malta from May until October. For any newly arrived pilots, this is where the third and last stage of their fighter training would take place. Replacement pilots would soon learn about the squadron's tactics and fighting discipline as taught at squadron-level by individual commanders. The level of tuition would vary from squadron to squadron depending on the time available and the skill and patience of each individual squadron commander. The CO of 360ª *Squadriglia*, Capitano Carlo Miani, taught his charges well for the unit did not suffer a single fatality during the Malta campaign in 1942.
(Giorgio Apostolo)

Beurling's first victim was Sergente Maggiore Francesco Pecchiari of 352ª *Squadriglia*, 20° *Gruppo*, who survived and was picked up from the sea. The Canadian claimed that his second victim was also a C.202:

> The same performance followed with another Macchi. Like the first one, this baby picked on 'Smitty', and I on 'Smitty's' friend. He saw me coming, however, and broke away diving. We were down vertically together from 20,000ft to about 5,000ft, and I let him have it just as he pulled out, from about 300 yards and slightly to starboard.'

Beurling's opponent was in fact an Re.2001 from 152ª *Squadriglia*. At the same time the Macchi pilots of 151ª *Squadriglia* reported contact with the Spitfires of No. 249 Sqn, Capitano Furio Doglio Niclot claiming one shot down – the RAF unit suffered no losses, however.

On the final raid of the day Beurling was once again scrambled (in BR323/S). His third victim would be a Bf 109. Incredibly, Beurling would catch his quarry with a full deflection shot from 800 yards! This third kill made Beurling an ace – he had claimed two Fw 190s in May with No. 41 Sqn on the Channel front. Multi-victory missions would become the norm for Beurling, for on 12 July he would be credited with two C.202s and a Re.2001 destroyed, followed by two C.202s 15 days later for his last victories over the type.

Beurling was not the only pilot to claim multiple victories during combat over Malta, however. Capitano Furio Doglio Niclot would shoot down another Spitfire and share in the destruction of a second one on 10 July, followed by two shot down and one damaged three days later.

By mid July the Italian offensive against Malta had run out of steam. Their bombers stopped appearing over the island and their fighter force was struggling to keep sufficient aircraft serviceable to sustain a heightened tempo of operations. Nevertheless, C.202 units continued to engage RAF fighters, and on 27 July they were dealt a demoralizing blow.

Thirteen *Folgores* (11 from 20° *Gruppo* and two from 155° *Gruppo*) were assigned as indirect escort for nine Ju 88s. Twenty-two Spitfires from Nos. 185, 249 and 126 Sqns were scrambled to intercept the formation, and as they began their attacks on the Ju 88s the Italian fighter pilots attempted to help the bombers. No. 249 Sqn spotted the Macchis approaching, and Sgt Beurling (in BR301/UF-S) latched onto

Capitano Furio Doglio Niclot's C.202 MM9043 '151-1', which he flew in action over Malta. Note the rare white command pennant forward of 51° Stormo's famous 'black cat and green mice' emblem. Due to the short distance (60 miles) between Sicily and Malta, most C.202 pilots would fly their aircraft without a full fuel load. The trade off was better performance once in aerial combat. Capitano Niclot achieved six victories over Malta while flying this aircraft before being shot down in it by Sgt George Beurling on 27 July 1942. (Giorgio Apostolo)

a C.202 and with a straight deflection shot hit its engine and radiator. His victim was Sergente Maggiore Falerio Gelli of 378ª *Squadriglia* (who had himself claimed three Malta Spitfires destroyed).

As he had done so many times before, Beurling methodically moved onto his next target and opened fire. 'The poor devil simply blew to pieces in the air'. His victim was none other than Capitano Furio Doglio Niclot, the leading Italian ace of Malta. His fighter had been mortally hit and it crashed into the sea before Niclot could bail out. For the Italians it was body blow. Squadronmate Ronaldo Scaroni recalled:

> When he died, some of the fighting spirit of the *Regia Aeronautica* died with him. There was a feeling that if Furio Doglio Niclot couldn't survive, none of us could. For the first time we began to doubt that Malta could be taken.

Not only did the Italians lose one of their leading aces, the low serviceability rates of the C.202 forced them to cease all operations at the end of the month.

Between 6 and 29 July 'Screwball' Beurling had been be credited with six C.202s, three Re.2001s and six Bf 109s.

October would see a renewed effort by both the *Regia Aeronautica* and the Luftwaffe in what would ultimately prove to be the final attempt made by the Axis powers to neutralize Malta. The Italians would muster close to 100 C.202s from 51° and 53° *Stormi*, with the Germans adding 58 serviceable Bf 109F-4s and G-2s to the fighter force. The RAF could now respond with 113 Spitfire Vs and 100 combat-hardened pilots. Invading Malta was

The C.202 of Sgt George Beurling's 13th victim, Sergente Maggiore Faliero Gelli of 378ª *Squadriglia*, 155° *Gruppo*, 51° *Stormo*. He survived his crash landing near Victoria, capital of Gozo, on 27 July 1942 and was pulled from the fighter in an unconscious state after smashing his face on the instrument panel when he hit the ground. Of this action Beurling wrote, 'It was a straight deflection shot that went into his engine and radiator. He flicked into a spin but managed to pull out, crash-landing on Gozo'. (Author)

During a pause in the action members of No. 249 Sqn pose for the camera at Takali in August 1942. They are, front row from left to right, Plt Offs A. S. Yates, H. H. Moody and R. P. Round, Flg Off Lodge (Intelligence Officer), Flt Lt E. L. Hetherington, Wg Cdr J. M. Thompson (Takali Wing leader), Sqn Ldr R. A. Mitchell, Gp Capt W. K. Le May (Station Commander), Wg Cdr A. H. Donaldson (deputy Takali Wing leader), Flt Lts L. W. Watts and F. E. Jones and Plt Offs Seldon (Intelligence Officer), J. Lowery, O. M. Linton and C. S. G. De Nancrede. In the back row, again from left to right, are Flt Sgt J. G. Sanderson, Sgt M. I. Gass, Flt Sgt N. M. Park (No. 126 Sqn), Sgt V. H. Wynn, Sgt W. S. Shewell, Sgt R. W. Lamont, Flt Sgt B. Butler, Plt Off J. W. Williams, Flt Sgts L. G. C. de l'Ara and G. F. Beurling, Flt Lt A. F. Roscoe (No. 229 Sqn), Plt Off J. G. W. Farmer (No. 229 Sqn), Flt Sgt E. T. Hiskens, Sgt A. E. Budd, Plt Off R. Seed and Flt Sgt Morgan (groundcrew NCO). Note the 51° *Stormo* emblem in front of Sqn Ldr Mitchell and Gp Capt Le May, which had been souvenired from a downed C.202. (Author)

now clearly out of the question, but if Rommel's forces in Africa were to prevail, the threat posed by the island had to be nullified.

The so-called 'October Blitz' commenced on the 11th and would end one week later. During the nine days of attacks the *Regia Aeronautica* and the Luftwaffe mounted approximately 2,400 sorties (the majority being flown by fighters) and dropped 440 tons of bombs. No airfields were put out of action for longer than 30 minutes, and on average 74 Spitfires were ready each day to oppose the Axis attackers. The RAF fighters exacted a heavy toll too, with 30 aircraft and 14 pilots being lost. For the rest of the month the *Regia Aeronautica* and the Luftwaffe reverted to fighter sweeps and small-scale fighter-bomber raids using bomb-carrying Re.2001s and Bf 109s. These missions were more nuisance than effective. The last C.202 to be shot down over Malta fell on 24 October to Plt Off Mike Giddings (BR565/T) of No. 249 Sqn, who recalled:

I attacked one gaggle of Macchis in line astern, when the last three rolled onto their backs and dived down. I fired at the No. 3 aircraft of the remainder with cannon and machine guns for about three seconds. Glycol poured from it and there was a violent explosion around the cockpit and the fuselage broke up.

The last significant raid involving C.202s over Malta occurred three days later when, at 1015 hrs, six *Jabos* escorted by about 60 C.202s and Bf 109s attacked Luqa airfield. Spitfires from Nos. 126 and 229 Sqns scrambled to engage the enemy aircraft but no interception was made.

By the end of October the siege of Malta was all but over. The defenders had weathered a number of storms and the RAF claims for October were as follows – 126 confirmed victories (of which 17 were C.202s), 62 probables (three being C.202s) and 162 damaged (18 being C.202s).

Operation *Torch* and the invasion of Tunisia and Algeria on 8 November 1942 sealed the fate of the Axis forces in the Mediterranean. Forced to urgently send reinforcements to North Africa, the fighter pilots of the *Regia Aeronautica* soon found themselves fighting against overwhelming odds in a struggle they knew would only end in defeat.

STATISTICS AND ANALYSIS

Often described as 'the fighter pilot's paradise' and 'no place for beginners', the air battles over Malta rank as the most intense of World War II. As well a creating no fewer than 34 aces for the RAF in 1942 alone, it would forever cement the legend of the Spitfire in the history of aerial warfare. In just over two-and-a-half years of combat it had saved Britain twice from complete catastrophe.

In terms of fighter-versus-fighter combat no two aircraft were as evenly matched as the Spitfire V and the C.202. But this is where the simple numbers (airspeed, rate-of-climb and manoeuvrability) fall by the wayside. Just two C.202 pilots became aces over Malta during 1942! The reasons for this are many and varied. While the *Folgore* was one of the best fighters of World War II, its performance alone was not enough. The production rate of the C.202 was very low, which meant the *Regia Aeronautica* could never fully convert its fighter force to the *Folgore*.

Serviceability was also a major issue. Indeed, when the *Regia Aeronautica* had to suspend all fighter operations due to a lack of serviceable aircraft at the end of July, it virtually took away any chance that would-be aces had to add to their scores. Aircraft availability also tied directly into sortie rates. While Italian pilots might fly one or two missions a day, the British would often fly two or three, and one of the biggest determining factors in becoming an ace was opportunity. Malta was a target-rich environment, but it was much richer for the British. While the Italians might send 20 to 30 C.202s on a mission (along with up to 40 Bf 109s from the Luftwaffe), the RAF would usually only scramble between 12 and 25 Spitfires.

OVERLEAF
23 June 1942 would see considerable action over Malta. At 1750hrs 12 Spitfires from No. 249 Sqn and eight from No. 603 Sqn were scrambled from Takali. The incoming raid consisted of three S.84s escorted by 27 C.202s of 155° *Gruppo*. As the Spitfires from No. 249 Sqn went for the bombers, No. 603 Sqn took on the fighter escort. Flg Off Wally McLeod of the latter unit, flying Spitfire VC X-B (serial unknown), spotted 12 Macchis west of Gozo and dove into the attack from 29,000ft. Damaging one C.202 with a short burst from 100 yards, he gave chase to another. After a long dogfight, and closing in to just 25 yards, McLeod fired a short burst that sent the C.202 diving into the sea from 5,000ft — reportedly 'out of panic' according to the future Canadian ace, this *Folgore* being his first of 21 victories. McLeod would eventually be credited with three C.202s shot down and two damaged, making him Malta's second highest-scoring Spitfire ace against the C.202. He would be credited with 13 victories in total over Malta.

Plt Off John 'Slim' Yarra of No. 185 Sqn was the highest scoring Australian ace over Malta in 1942. Seated here in his personally marked Spitfire (BR387/GL-W), he claimed 12 enemy aircraft destroyed (including three C.202s), 2 probables and 6 damaged whilst defending the island. (Frederick Galea)

One of the leading RAF aces in the early years of the war, Bill Rolls already had 8.5 kills to his name when he flew off HMS Furious for Malta on 11 August 1942 during the Pedestal operation. Once on the island he was made a flight commander in No. 126 Sqn. Rolls was subsequently credited with a further nine victories during his time on Malta, including two C.202s and a Ju 88 on 12 October. (via Frederick Galea)

For Spitfire pilots, their scores are much higher, which is a remarkable achievement considering the environment in which they had to fight. Their bases were bombed day and night, resulting in precious Spitfires being destroyed on the ground as well as in the air. Scrambles were constant, with little time for relief between raids. The diet endured by the pilots was meagre, and dysentery and illness were rife. The physical and psychological toll was immense, but they had little choice but to cope with it, for every pilot was needed. What they did have in their favour, however, was excellent leadership, battle-tested tactics and a strong belief in what they were doing. Radar would also play a vital role. Being able to vector intercepting fighters directly onto approaching bomber formations at the correct altitude gave British pilots a vital advantage. Indeed, without it the battle would have been lost. The skills of the various fighter controllers was well respected, as Plt Off Philip Dixon of No. 229 Sqn recalled:

It was remarkable how on many occasions the controllers were able to interpret their plots to such a high degree that they could differentiate between an ordinary fighter formation and a fighter-bomber formation. The information that we were given by the controllers was, of course, invaluable and very reassuring, both from the point of knowing where your enemy was coming from, and what he was using in the way of aircraft. Furthermore, it was also heartening to know that you would probably be plotted if you had to force land in the sea.

The Italians, on the other hand, did not have the advantage of radar. To compensate the *Regia Aeronautica* developed a highly advanced radio interception apparatus that allowed communications between RAF aircraft and their ground bases to be intercepted and monitored. Receiver–transmitter stations, set up at airfields throughout Sicily, would be in voice contact with the fighters in the air. It was only partially successful, however, and was no match for the British radar and fighter control system in place on Malta.

As the island's greatest defender, George Beurling had no peer with 29.333 victories to his name by the time he was shot down and wounded on 14 October. What is remarkable about Beurling's total was the number of multiple victories he would score on single missions. Most pilots would be happy to score just one, but Beurling's skills put him in a league of his own. It must also be noted that the majority of his victories were over fighters. And these aircraft were also the best the Axis had to offer at the time in-theatre, being equal to or better than the Spitfire V. Not only did he shoot down six C.202s, he would also claim three Re.2001s and 15 Bf 109s. All three fighters types had one thing in common – they were powered by a version of the DB 601 engine. The C.202 and Re.2001 were fitted with the DB 601A-1 while the Bf 109F-4 had the slightly more powerful DB 601E.

Next in line in terms of C.202 victories was Beurling's fellow countryman Flt Lt Henry Wallace McLeod, who flew initially with No. 603 Sqn before being transferred to No. 1435 Sqn. He would score 13 victories over Malta during 1942, three of them

C.202s (with two more damaged). McLeod would later be killed in action over Arnhem on 27 September 1944, by which point his tally stood at 21 destroyed, 3 probables, 12 damaged and 1 shared damaged.

Considering all the disadvantages the Italians faced and the limited firepower of their aircraft, a handful of C.202 pilots had nevertheless fared well over Malta. The most successful pilot of 1942 was Furio Doglio Niclot of 51° *Stormo*, whose six and three shared Spitfires destroyed was closely followed by Ennio Tarantola with five and three shared Spitfires destroyed. Both were members of 51° *Stormo*, the *Regia Aeronautica's* top-scoring unit over Malta with 97 aircraft claimed destroyed. The two top scoring Italian aces of the war also added to their scores while flying over Malta with 4° *Stormo*, Teresio Martinoli claiming three Spitfire victories during 1942 (he was the ranking Italian ace of the war with 22 victories to his name) and Franco Lucchini claiming two (he was credited with 21 victories in World War II and one in Spain).

While many aces had been created over Malta, a significant number of pilots had lost their lives too. No fewer than 102 Spitfire pilots would be killed in 1942 – 45 from Britain, 20 Canadians, 12 New Zealanders, ten Australians, ten Americans, three Rhodesians, a South African and a Frenchman. From March to November 148 Spitfires were lost in the air, 66 force-landed or crash-landed and five were destroyed on the ground. For the fighter pilots of the *Regia Aeronautica*, they would pay a particularly high price. While credited with fewer victories (Italian claims on occasion were extremely excessive, with pilots being credited with 100+ Spitfires shot down between May and the end of July alone!), and seeing only limited action over Malta, the *Regia Aeronautica* would lose at least 60 C.202s and Re.2001s, with 39 pilots killed.

From the British perspective it was the defensive battles that produced the largest number of aces during the war. Fighting a mass of enemy aircraft gave them plenty of targets to choose from. Flying over their own territory also gave Spitfire pilots the opportunity to bail out over or crash land on friendly territory and quickly return to the fray. The distance to and from the fighting area was short (this was also the case for the Italians, as the southern coast of Sicily was just 60 miles from Malta), giving pilots more time to engage enemy aircraft. But the defenders of Malta also faced some disadvantages, as they were usually outnumbered and forced to engage an enemy that enjoyed a height advantage.

In the end, the Spitfire V and C.202 were so evenly matched that victory often came down to a number of battle-proven variables. Here, the RAF had the upper hand. Its excellent radar and fighter control, matched with superior tactics, leadership, better armament in the Spitfire V and individual pilot skills, gave the Allies an advantage the Italians were hard-pressed to counter. The C.202 proved to be an excellent fighter, but its impact was less than desired. Production rates were extremely low (entire frontline units were still flying the C.200 well into 1943), and when the fighter did become operational serviceability rates were poor due to inadequate manufacturing methods and a lack of spare parts. Mario Castoldi's C.202 was a great fighter. Fortunately for the Allies it was never part of a effective fighter force.

Italy's second-highest scoring ace over Malta during 1942 was Maresciallo Ennio Tarantola, seen here pointing to his seven claims painted on the tail of his aircraft, MM9066 '2' of 151ª *Squadriglia*, 20° *Gruppo*. Flying from Gela airfield as wingman for Capitano Furio Doglio Niclot, Tarantola would claim five and three shared destroyed over Malta. Unlike his squadron commander, Tarantola survived the battles over Malta and would continue fighting from Sardinia in May 1943, claiming two P-38s shot down on 2 August. Following the armistice he joined the ANR and was shot down on 25 April 1944 by Thunderbolts from the 325th FG while flying his G.55 fighter. Tarantola would end the war with ten victories, plus one from his service in Spain. (Giorgio Apostolo)

Leading Spitfire V C.202 Killers Over Malta			
Name	**Unit(s)**	**C.202 Claims**	**Total Victories**
George Beurling RAF	No. 249 Sqn	6 C.202s destroyed	31.333
Henry McLeod RCAF	Nos. 603 and 1435 Sqns	3 C.202s destroyed and 2 damaged	21
John Yarra RAAF	No. 185 Sqn	3 C.202s destroyed	12
William Rolls RAF	No. 126 Sqn	2 C.202s destroyed	17.5
Kenneth Evans RAF	No. 126 Sqn	2 C.202s destroyed	5
James Ballantyne RCAF	Nos. 603 and 229 Sqns	2 C.202s destroyed	5
Lawrence Verrall RNZAF	No. 249 Sqn	2 C.202s destroyed	3
Maurice Stephens RAF	Nos. 249 and 229 Sqns	1.5 C.202s destroyed	22
Colin Parkinson RAAF	Nos. 603 and 229 Sqns	1.333 C.202s destroyed and 2 damaged	8.5
Eric Hetherington RAF	No. 249 Sqn	1.333 C.202s destroyed	3.333
William Walton RAF	No. 1435 Sqn	1 C.202 destroyed, 1 probable and 2 damaged	6
John Plagis RAF	Nos. 249 and 185 Sqns	1 C.202 destroyed and 1 damaged	16
John McElroy RCAF	No. 249 Sqn	1 C.202 destroyed and 1 damaged	11 plus 3 postwar
George Buchanan RAF	No. 249 Sqn	1 C.202 destroyed	6.5
Ian Maclennan RAF	No. 1435 Sqn	1 C.202 destroyed	7
Claude Weaver RCAF	No. 185 Sqn	1 C.202 destroyed	12.5
Patrick Schade RAF	No. 126 Sqn	1 C.202 destroyed	13.5
John Bisley RAAF	No. 126 Sqn	1 C.202 destroyed	6.5
Ripley Jones RCAF	No. 126 Sqn	1 C.202 damaged	8
Adrian Goldsmith RAAF	No. 126	1 C.202 damaged	16.5
Arthur Varey RAF	No. 126	1 C.202 damaged	5.5
Eric Woods RAF	No. 249 Sqn	1 C.202 destroyed on ground, 1 probable and 1 damaged	11

ENGAGING THE ENEMY

During the defence of Malta the Spitfire's armament consisted of two Hispano Mk II 20mm cannon and four Browning 0.303-in. machine guns. While the initial Mk VC Trops had been delivered with a four cannon arrangement, two of the weapons were soon taken out due to frequent jamming caused by faulty ammunition. Pilots also noted an improved performance with two of the cannons removed. The cannon had a useful range of 600 yards for air-to-air fighting, with a total firing time of between ten and twelve seconds, while the machine guns could be fired for a further five seconds. The low weight-of-fire and slight penetration of the 0.303-in. shells meant that pilots had to open fire at extremely close range to do any serious damage. While the Spitfire is regarded as one of the best fighters of World War II,

there is good reason to infer that it was not the best gun platform. Weapons that were easily harmonized when jacked up in the hangar would be subject to a number of twisting forces while airborne. Propeller torque, engine vibration and the lightness of the Spitfire's structure led to torsional flexing of the fuselage and flying surfaces. At high power settings precise sighting would be lost, along with the ability to score first-round strikes at ranges beyond 200 yards. Weapon harmonization was also an issue, as the machine guns were not harmonized with the cannon. Rather than being set to converge at a point ahead of the gunsight (a Barr and Stroud GM 2 reflector unit, as fitted to the Spitfire I from 1939), they were aligned to fill a volume of air in front of the fighter with as much lead as possible.

Maresciallo Pasquale Bartolucci of 51° *Stormo* poses in front of his C.202. He and his unit would see action over Malta between June and October 1942, Bartolucci claiming two Spitfires shot down during this period. He finished the war with four personal and two shared victories to his name. (Giorgio Apostolo)

Leading C.202 Spitfire V Killers Over Malta			
Name	**Unit**	**Spitfire Claims**	**Total Victories**
Furio Doglio Niclot	51° *Stormo*	6 destroyed and 3 shared destroyed	7.5
Ennio Tarantola	51° *Stormo*	5 destroyed and 3 shared destroyed	10 plus 1 in Spain

It must be acknowledged that the scores attributed to Niclot and his wingman Tarantola are not definitive, and the numbers quoted should be treated as claims and not 'confirmed' kills. While pilots were permitted to report claims in their personal logbooks, official accreditation was given to the unit, making individual scores hard to compile. Over the years extensive research done by authors Giovanni Massimello, Giorgio Apostolo, Christopher Shores, Brian Cull and Nicola Malizia has resulted in what is considered to be the most accurate listing of Italian aces of World War II.

AFTERMATH

It was a lost opportunity. The attempt made by the *Regia Aeronautica* and Luftwaffe to neutralize Malta was a classic example of air power not being fully realized. Many times during the siege the Axis air forces were able to gain clear air superiority over the island, but they never exploited their advantage either through a full-scale invasion or a complete blockade. Supplies still got through, and with the arrival of Spitfires from March 1942 the defences were considerably improved.

The reasons behind the Axis Powers' inability to neutralize Malta completely were many and varied. Firstly, there was the geography of Malta itself. The island is essentially one giant rock, which meant that the high-explosive bombs used by German and Italian aircraft in their attempt to destroy the RAF's airfields were ineffective as they expended most of their energy upwards and outwards when they detonated. Against the hard surface of Malta these weapons proved futile. While a great number of aircraft were destroyed on the ground, the airfields were never knocked out. This was due in part to the work performed by the British Army. The RAF had access to heavy equipment and hundreds of soldiers who could operate it, and it was their job to effect quick runway repairs.

Secondly, the Axis was also unable to stop supplies and reinforcements from reaching the island. The fact that 367 Spitfires were flown in is testament to that fact. This stands in stark contrast to the *Regia Aeronautica's* inability to field more than 60 to 100 C.202s (these numbers were usually lower due to unserviceablility) at any one time. The *Regia Aeronautica*, like the Luftwaffe, was overstretched and committed on too many fronts. Just when they came close to neutralizing the island in the early spring of 1942, campaigns on other fronts (the Eastern Front and the offensive in North Africa) took priority, shifting forces away from Malta. This allowed the British to regroup and grow stronger. It also revealed the *Regia Aeronautica's* crippling weaknesses. While its

When the armistice was publicly announced on 8 September 1943 the *Regia Aeronautica* was caught by surprise. Each unit reacted differently, with some joining the Germans while others, including 270 pilots who flew south, sided with the Allies. At the time just 16 C.202s were ready for combat with the newly formed *Aeronautica Co-Belligerante*, which meant groundcrews had to scour the battlefields of North Africa, Sicily, Sardinia and southern Italy for spare parts, fuel and aircraft. These C.202s, abandoned amongst the cacti in Tunisia, have clearly been scavenged for usable parts by the Italians and souvenirs for the victorious Allies – the *Regia Aeronautica*'s 'Stemma Sabaudo' emblem has been carefully cut out of the rudder of each fighter. (Author)

airmen were brave and dedicated to their task, they never had the numbers or the right kind of bombers to take on the task alone.

The Spitfire V and C.202 would continue to meet in combat after the 'October Blitz'. Operation *Torch* and the Allied invasion of Tunisia and Algeria on 8 November 1942 all but ended enemy air activity over Malta. As soon as airfields could be secured in North Africa the RAF flew in seven units of Spitfire Vs (Nos. 72, 81, 93, 11, 152, 154 and 242 Sqns). The USAAF also contributed the Spitfire V-equipped 31st and 52nd Fighter Groups. Italian and German forces in North Africa were now facing total destruction. The *Regia Aeronautica* rushed what remaining C.202s it could spare to North Africa to help stem the tide, and by 21 February 1943 just 55 *Folgores* were serviceable on Sicily, split between 6° and 16° *Gruppi*.

The Allied victory in North Africa on 13 May 1943 led directly to the invasion of Sicily (Operation *Husky*) on 10 July. Malta, located just 60 miles from Sicily, would play a major role in the invasion, with 23 squadrons of Spitfires providing both fighter and fighter-bomber support. Although several units had re-equipped with the more powerful Spitfire VIII and IX by then, the Mk V still remained the most numerous RAF fighter type in-theatre.

In response to the impending invasion the *Regia Aeronautica* prepared its defence of the island. On the eve of *Husky*, the Italians could muster 359 airworthy aircraft, of which approximately 67 were C.202s – there were also a small number of newer C.205V *Veltros* available too. Outnumbered and outgunned, the C.202 pilots fought a losing battle. By 17 August the battle for Sicily was over and the bombing of mainland Italy increased in tempo. The fall of Sicily and the bombing of Rome ultimately led to the dismissal of Benito Mussolini and a signed armistice with the Allies on 3 September 1943. A painful and humiliating split in the *Regia Aeronautica* duly followed, which resulted in Italy being the only nation during World War II to have separate air forces fighting for each side.

In the south the *Aeronautica Co-Belligerante* was formed, but it suffered from a serious shortage of aircraft. At the time of the armistice there were just 200 C.202s in Italy and Sardinia, of which 93 *Folgores* and a small number of C.205Vs found themselves within the ranks of the *Aeronautica Co-Belligerante*. Of that total just 16 C.202s were ready for combat. By October 1943 21° *Gruppo*, 5° *Stormo* had managed to up its strength to 24 *Folgores*. In May 1944 the Allies agreed to re-equip the Italians with more modern aircraft types, and in an ironic twist 20° *Gruppo*, 51° *Stormo* received 53 ex-RAF Spitfire

VBs and Cs from Nos. 249 and 352 Sqns. The first Italian Spitfire sortie of the war was a reconnaissance mission flown over Yugoslavia on 23 October.

In the north the C.202 would play a lesser role as part of the newly formed fascist *Aeronautica Nazionale Repubblicana* (ANR). For the majority of the pilots serving with the *Regia Aeronautica* in northern Italy at the time of the armistice there was little choice but to continue flying alongside the Luftwaffe. Admittedly, some volunteered for the ANR while others escaped to the south, but for the majority they had no option but to fly. The alternative was to face deportation to a German labour camp.

In September 1943 there were some 50 C.202s in the north. These aircraft were interned by the Germans and allocated to units of the ANR. Most were used for training and point defence of industry and aerodromes.

The only other air arm to use the C.202 during World War II was the Croatian Air Force Legion. From January 1944 it received eight brand new C.202s, followed by four more two weeks later. It is estimated the Croats ultimately received 20 to 22 C.202s.

The Spitfire V would continue flying well into 1944. By the time of the D-Day landings on 6 June 1944, nine squadrons of LF Vs were assigned to the Air Defence of Great Britain and two squadrons to the Air Spotting Pool. By the end of the war the Mk V had all but disappeared from frontline service (except for in modified Seafire L III and F III form, these aircraft effectively being Spitfire Vs equipped with an arrestor hook). Replaced by the Mks VIII, IX and Griffon-powered XIV, the Spitfire V will forever be remembered for the crucial role it played in the defence of Malta during 1942.

For the Italian armed forces the war had been a disaster. Their contribution has often been portrayed in history books as cowardly and incompetent and their equipment described as obsolete and inferior. It must be remembered that the bulk of Rommel's famed *Africa Korps* was made up of Italian troops. And although the Bf 109 is often described as being the sole Axis fighter encountered during the aerial battles over Malta and North Africa during the pivotal year of 1942, the truth is that the C.202 was constantly present throughout. Belittled by the Allies during the war for the purposes of propaganda, the C.202 *Folgore* represented the best in Italian fighter design during the conflict. Renowned for its finger-light handling, it was superior to the Hurricane, Tomahawk and Kittyhawk and equal to or better than the Spitfire V. While the C.202 may have had excellent performance, its combat capability never matched that of the Spitfire V, however.

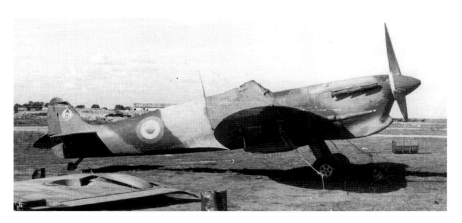

Once foe now friend, this ex-RAF Spitfire VC Trop – photographed here at Galatina parked alongside the damaged wing of a Spitfire – was one of 53 ex-RAF Supermarine fighters issued to 20° *Gruppo*, 51° *Stormo* of the *Aeronautica Co-Belligerante* in October 1944. Their first mission took place on the 24th of that month when the Spitfires undertook armed reconnaissance sweeps over German-held Yugoslavia. (Richard J. Caruana)

FURTHER READING

BOOKS

Apostolo, Giorgio, *Wings of Italy – The Italian Air Force in Original World War II Colour Pictures* (GAE, Milan, 1993)

Barber, Mark, *Warrior 164: RAF Fighter Command Pilot – The Western Front 1939–42* (Osprey Publishing, Oxford, 2012)

Beurling, George F., and Roberts, Leslie, *Malta Spitfire* (Oxford University Press, Toronto, 1943)

Cull, Brian, *Spitfires Over Malta – The Epic Air Battles of 1942* (Grub Street, London, 2005)

Dunning, Chris, *Regia Aeronautica – The Italian Air Force 1923–1945 – An Operational Record* (Chevron Publishing Limited, Surrey, 2009)

Green, William, *Warplanes of the Second World War – Fighters Volume Two* (MacDonald & Co, London, 1961)

Green, William, *Famous Fighters of the Second World War* (Doubleday & Company, New York, 1962)

Grinker, Roy R. and Spiegel, John P., *Men Under Stress* (McGraw-Hill Book Co. Inc., New York, 1963)

Gunston, Bill, *Classic World War II Aircraft Cutaways* (Osprey Publishing, London, 1995)

Holmes, Tony, *Duel 5: Spitfire vs Bf 109 – Battle of Britain* (Osprey Publishing, Oxford, 2007)

Massimello, Giovanni and Apostolo, Giorgio, *Aircraft of the Aces 34: Italian Aces of World War 2* (Osprey Publishing, Oxford, 2000)

McKinstry, Leo, *Portrait of a Legend – Spitfire* (John Murray Publishers, London, 2008)

Morgan, Hugh and Seibel, Jurgen, *Combat Kill* (Patrick Stephens Limited, Somerset, 1997)

Nichols, Steve, *Aircraft of the Aces 83: Malta Spitfire Aces* (Osprey Publishing, Oxford, 2008)

Price, Dr Alfred, *Aircraft of the Aces 16: Spitfire Mark V Aces 1941–45* (Osprey Publishing, London, 1997)

Ralph, Wayne, *Aces, Warriors and Wingmen* (John Wiley & Sons, Mississauga, 2005)

Shacklady, Edwin and Morgan, Eric, *Spitfire – The History* (Key Books Ltd, Stamford, 2000)

Shores, Christopher and Cull, Brian, *Malta: The Spitfire Year 1942* (Grub Street, London, 2002)

Shores, Christopher and Williams, Clive, *Aces High* (Grub Street, London, 1994)

Shores, Christopher, *Aces High Volume 2* (Grub Street, London, 1999)

Shores, Christopher, *Those Other Eagles* (Grub Street, London 2004)

Skulski, Przemystaw, *Macchi C.202 Folgore* (Stratus, Warsaw, 2012)

WEBSITES

www.spitfireperformance.com
www.spitfiresite.com

INDEX